Radical Nonintervention

EDWIN M. SCHUR

is Professor and Head of the Department of Sociology at New York University. Among his other books are *Crimes Without Victims—Deviant Behavior and Public Policy; Abortion, Homosexuality, and Drug Addiction;* and *Our Criminal Society: The Social and Legal Sources of Crime in America.*

RADICAL NONINTERVENTION
rethinking the delinquency problem

. . . Edwin M. Schur . . .

PRENTICE-HALL, INC. A SPECTRUM BOOK Englewood Cliffs, N.J.

Library of Congress Cataloging in Publication Data

SCHUR, EDWIN M
   Radical nonintervention.

   (A Spectrum Book)
   Includes bibliographical references.
    1. Juvenile delinquency—United States.
2. Rehabilitation of juvenile delinquents—United
States. 3. Social work with delinquents and
criminals—United States. I. Title.
HV9104.S328   364.36′0973   73–1282
ISBN 0–13–750422–5
ISBN 0–13–750414–4 (pbk)

•

10 9 8 7 6 5 4 3 2 1

PRENTICE-HALL INTERNATIONAL, INC. (*London*)
PRENTICE-HALL OF AUSTRALIA PTY., LTD. (*Sydney*)
PRENTICE-HALL OF CANADA, LTD. (*Toronto*)
PRENTICE-HALL OF INDIA PRIVATE LIMITED (*New Delhi*)
PRENTICE-HALL OF JAPAN, INC. (*Tokyo*)

Contents

Preface   *ix*

RETHINKING THE DELINQUENCY PROBLEM   1

Central Value Concerns   5
Specialists, Policy-Makers, and the Public   7
Public Attitudes and Misconceptions   9
Delinquency Typologies   13
A New Approach   18

TREATING THE INDIVIDUAL   27

Theories and Methods   31
Predicting Delinquency   46
Behavior Modification   51
Counseling, Probation, and Community Treatment   54
Institutional Treatment   64
Individualized Justice   70

REFORMING SOCIETY   79

Theories and Methods   84
Street-Gang Work   94
Community Action Programs   102
General Social Reform   105
Socialized Justice   110

NEW WAYS OF LOOKING AT DELINQUENCY   115

Labeling Analysis   118
The Unmasking of Euphemism   126
The Organizational Factor   130
Organizational Needs   131
Neo-Antideterminism   135
Deviance and Politics   139
Limiting the Criminal Law   143

RADICAL NONINTERVENTION   151

Theories and Methods   155
Toward New Priorities   166

Index   *175*

Preface

The sociological data and theories relating to juvenile delinquency are extremely voluminous and very confusing. Work in this area is highly variable in quality and in style runs the full range from intricate statistical analysis of minute points to broad-scale interpretation. Theories contradict one another and data are inconsistent. To make some sense out of all this is no small task, and I do not delude myself that my own effort to do so is definitive. On the other hand, I believe that a focus on major reaction patterns does help pull these diverse materials together in a meaningful way, as well as providing a useful vantage point if one is concerned with issues of public policy. Such a framework may also be helpful for those not already well versed in the sociological literature of delinquency—to whom this work is directed.

This study was prepared for the Juvenile Justice Standards Project of the Institute of Judicial Administration at New York University Law School. The Project is supported by funds from the

National Institute of Law Enforcement and Criminal Justice, The Andrew W. Mellon Foundation, the American Bar Endowment, the Vincent Astor Foundation, and the Herman Goldman Foundation. In particular, a grant from the Herman Goldman Foundation enabled the Project to pursue the line of inquiry that resulted in this book. The views expressed herein and the recommendations advanced are, however, those of the author.

Paul Nejelski and Larry Schultz at the Project have been most helpful and encouraging, and I am grateful also to Kurt Schlichting of New York University for his able research assistance and to Michael Hunter, Edward Stanford, and Marjorie Streeter of Prentice-Hall for their interest and advice. Finally, I would like to thank Margarita Contreras, Justine Elliot, Shirley Fields, and Geraldine Novasic for their extremely competent typing of the manuscript.

Radical Nonintervention

RETHINKING THE DELINQUENCY PROBLEM

There is widespread agreement that our progress in achieving the stated goals of the juvenile justice system has been far from satisfactory. Indeed, according to one leading analyst, "Although the child savers were rhetorically concerned with protecting children from the physical and moral dangers of an increasingly industrialized and urban society, their remedies seemed to aggravate the problem." [1] Somehow, good intentions notwithstanding, the special mechanisms developed for dealing with young offenders on an individual basis and in a nonpunitive way have backfired. Most acute observers now express considerable disenchantment with the informal nonadversary procedures of the traditional juvenile court, the specialized and rehabilitation-oriented "treatment institutions," and the allegedly nonstigmatizing terminology of delinquency policies. The early criticisms of a small number of legal analysts are now voiced as well by social scientists (whose studies have revealed yet additional shortcomings of the system), and by nonacademics working in the field. In a recent survey of attitudes concerning delinquency causation and policies among staff members of the California Youth Authority, a solid majority of the respondents advocated, among other things, "a strong effort to divert more youth from the justice-correctional system—because of its potential for harm." [2]

A good deal of the dissatisfaction has focused on the failure to provide adequate legal safeguards and to develop and support efficient ways to enforce juvenile justice policies. These matters of procedure and administrative efficiency, while obviously central to any legal efforts to deal with youth problems, will not occupy us greatly in the present study. As we shall see below, however, a sociological analysis helps policy-makers even in these seemingly technical areas. It is worth emphasizing, in this connection, that the Supreme Court's 1967 decision in the *Gault* case (articulating constitutional requirements of due process in the juvenile court) was not grounded solely in legal considerations.[3] On the contrary, the Court's opinion drew substantially on an accumulated body of empirical knowledge about how the system of juvenile justice really worked.

This point is important because all too often conventional wisdom has decreed that the sociologist's role must be limited to conducting research on delinquency causation, whereas questions of program implementation must be addressed only by the policy-maker. Obviously, someone is going to have to make and enforce policy decisions, and ordinarily it will not be the sociologist. At the same time separating the causes of delinquency from other concerns of the juvenile justice system is arbitrary and unwarranted. Presumably, as most enlightened policy-makers themselves would insist, social science research and analysis on the "causes" of delinquency should help to provide a basis for measures aimed at prevention, treatment, and control. Similarly, there is a growing recognition of the important role the social scientist may play in evaluation. Subjective impressions are no longer sufficient to assess the effectiveness of delinquency programs. Instead, policy-makers increasingly demand systematic and carefully controlled evaluations that approximate an experimental design. And in the field of delinquency, as in other areas of social science, the notion of "action research"—in which implementing and evaluating the program proceed simultaneously—has gained considerable acceptance.

CENTRAL VALUE CONCERNS

While the influence of empirical research on delinquency policy may now be fairly apparent, delinquency research itself often presupposes a certain policy. Above all, in order to conduct research on the causes of delinquency, we must first clarify exactly what delinquency is. It is far from obvious. If we begin with the proposition that "delinquency is that behavior prohibited by the delinquency laws," [4] and assume for the moment that we can identify those statutes in any one jurisdiction that constitute "the delinquency laws", we confront the familiar cross-jurisdictional quagmire of inconsistent, vague, contradictory statutory provisions regarding youth offenses. Furthermore, as the President's Commission on Law Enforcement and Administration of Justice noted:

> In addition to behavior that would be criminal on the part of an adult, delinquency includes behavior illegal only for a child: Conduct uniquely children's—truancy, incorrigibility—and conduct tolerated for adults but objectionable for children—smoking, drinking, using vulgar language, violating curfew laws, hanging around in bars or with felons or gamblers.
>
> The provisions on which intervention in this category of cases is based are typically vague and all-encompassing: Growing up in idleness and crime, engaging in immoral conduct, in danger of leading an immoral life. Especially when administered with the informality characteristic of the court's procedures, they establish the judge as arbiter not only of the behavior but also of the morals of every child (and to an extent the parents of every child) appearing before him.[5]

We shall consider later the wisdom of such a broad jurisdiction for the court—which the Commission itself felt compelled to strongly dispute. For the present, we shall discuss a rather different and less obvious implication. Since delinquency is defined by statute, and few responsible commentators consider the current vague omnibus legal definitions to be socially reasonable or sociologically meaningful, then just what sort of behavior should concern the researcher seeking to understand delinquency's "causes"? In other words, if delinquency remains a highly elusive and ill-defined phenomenon, how can we really study it?

From a scientific standpoint, this lack of a precise definition poses methodological problems—some of which will be touched on below. Obviously, examining the causes of delinquency before defining it is a strange ordering of priorities. Any consideration of delinquency problems (even by researchers) requires an answer to a central, and all too often neglected question: Should there be a special category of behavior called "delinquency," and if so, what ought it to include?

This core concern is intentionally stated in normative, or value-choice, terms. Delinquency cannot simply be taken as a given to be studied and dealt with. On the contrary, it is a legislative and social construct, the nature and scope of which are subject to our determinations. True, removing the delinquency label from a type of behavior will not prevent its occurrence. Yet the use of the label (not only for particular kinds of behavior, but also as a broader designation) carries connotations that confuse the basic issues. Those who see delinquency as clearly existing "out there" also believe there is a distinct entity called "the delinquent." The delinquent is the "bad" child or youth. This implies that there must also be "good" or "normal" children. Offending behavior, then, is thought to be distributed quite unevenly throughout the young population and concentrated in a group of young wrongdoers. Major patterns of reaction to delinquency spring from variations on these and related assumptions.

As we shall see, many commentators now suggest that the delinquency label, if not useless, has been greatly overused. It has served as a convenient catchall that has enabled us to avoid openly facing our values when we assess problem behavior. It is much easier to call offenders "problem girls" or "female delinquents" than to carefully explore the meaning of adolescent sexuality and running away from home, and to think through just how we ought to respond to these actions. But in fact there is no way of fully avoiding the normative issue. To pretend to ignore the policy questions is simply to uphold, by failing to consider alternatives, whatever policies and responses currently prevail.

Not only our understanding of delinquency's causes, but also our programs for dealing with delinquency presuppose decisions on the appropriate scope of the delinquency laws. In order to know which specific delinquency programs we want to adopt, we must first have assessed the relative seriousness of the behavior. Value-choices, similarly, are a prerequisite for meaningful evaluation research—an area in which we might, at first glance, assume we confront a straightforward and merely technical question. Actually, asking whether a given program is effective involves more than simply asking a technical question. The criteria of effectiveness depend upon what the program goals are, and these goals are not nearly as self-evident as is supposed. The "effectiveness" of a program for gang members will depend on whether the primary goal is keeping them out of court, reducing their antisocial behavior, or pushing them into socially constructive activities.

SPECIALISTS, POLICY-MAKERS, AND THE PUBLIC

Given the emphasis on technology and expertise that pervades our culture, it is hardly surprising that the public and its elected representatives look to the specialist for "solutions" to delinquency problems. As I have said elsewhere,[6] it is characteristically American (perhaps because of our pragmatic ethos) to expect that an expert is going to score a "breakthrough" that will "cure" the problems of crime and delinquency. This belief in sudden technical solutions—together with the equally erroneous belief that there is really nothing at all we can do about crime—is highly unrealistic for several reasons. To begin with, a totally problemless society doesn't exist. Societies, virtually by definition, exhibit behavioral norms and violations of those norms. Indeed, as recent deviance theories emphasize, it is by the violations and the social reactions to them that members of the society maintain an adequate sense of what the norms are. From this standpoint, the total elimination of "crime" is not possible. (Nor, one might add, would it necessarily be desirable. Some aspects of what we now call "delinquency" may reflect a youthful diversity and a potential for innovation and cultural change that we might well wish to protect or even encourage.)

We cannot, then, expect to eliminate delinquency, but we can do a great deal to control, limit, and "shape" it. By developing a sound understanding of the behavior we call problematic, we can more meaningfully attack the roots of the "problem." We can also influence the "offenders" in various ways and ameliorate the general problem, although there is a growing belief that these measures are likely to have only a limited impact. And, because of the essentially legal nature of delinquency, we can alter the nature of delinquency problems somewhat by adjusting the scope of delinquency laws, perhaps even to the point, as we shall see, of completely eliminating "delinquency" as a formal and separate legal category. This measure, while not primarily affecting youthful behavior, would nonetheless have potentially far-reaching effects on its meaning and consequences in our society.

The sociologist cannot provide answers to the central value questions that pervade this field. Furthermore, the citizen or legislator who relegates this moral burden to the specialist evades his own responsibility. While the scientist cannot "prove" values, he has the freedom in his role as citizen, to state his own views. Hopefully, his views in his area of expertise will be highly informed, and the evidence he accumulates and develops through his research and analysis will help provide a sound basis for others' value-judgments. Yet there is no reason why his value-judgments, as such, should determine public policy. The specialist, therefore, should disabuse the public and the policy-makers of the notion that he has, or can have, all the answers.

On the other hand, the social scientist may evade *his* social responsibility if he insists that his professional work is completely free of value-judgments. It is an illusion to believe he can examine social issues without making any implicit value-judgments, especially in his selection of topics for investigation in the first place, and his decisions on the uses to which research findings may be put.

Until recently, sociologists have not directly considered policy issues on crime and delinquency. The general sociological neglect of law and legal institutions reflected a desire for scientific status; sociologists carefully avoided normative realms and concentrated on "empirical" investigations in order to be like the natural scientists.[7] One of sociology's most impressive early contributions was to reveal the largely hidden informal mechanisms of social control that govern group interactions; but by emphasizing this informal side of social life, it slighted more formalized mechanisms such as the law. Law was seen as a reflection of and reaction to social values and behavior patterns (that is, as a dependent variable) rather than as having in its own right some positive impact on the social order. Recent uses of law as a conscious instrument for the promotion of social change (as in racial desegregation and equal opportunity policies) helped produce a rethinking of this passive concept of law. But in the area of crime and delinquency analysis, it has taken sociologists a long time to heed the wisdom of Hermann Mannheim's sensible comment:

> We have made considerable efforts to discover what sort of person the offender is and why he has broken the law, and we rack our brains to find out what to do with him. . . . Hardly ever do we pause for a moment to examine critically the contents of that very law the existence of which alone makes it possible for the individual to offend against it.[8]

When we examine below some of the major recent trends in deviance theory, it will become clear that a developing emphasis on societal reactions to rule-breaking has served to focus new attention on both the substance of the criminal law and the administration of criminal justice.

PUBLIC ATTITUDES AND MISCONCEPTIONS

While few delinquency researchers would claim to have "solved" the problem behavior of youth, collectively they have managed to produce a large body of factual information and generate some useful perspectives on and theories about it.

One crucial area that has not, however, received adequate research attention is that of public beliefs and attitudes regarding delinquency. By and large, our knowledge of public information about delinquency and delinquency policies has been extremely sketchy; the same is true of data on how the public feels we should address these problems. If, as I have suggested, the public definition of delinquency is central to our understanding, then the investigation of public attitudes is especially crucial. As a leading legal analyst of juvenile justice problems has noted, "the question, What sorts of behavior should be declared criminal? is one to which the behavioral sciences might contribute vital insights. This they have largely failed to do, and we are the poorer for it." [9] Attitudinal research is especially significant because in the area of criminal justice there is a strong tendency to make assumptions about the nature of "public opinion" on various issues. Cautious legislators often assert that "the public would never countenance" innovative and experimental policies. Findings from carefully conducted attitude research may reveal that such assumptions are partially or totally unwarranted; or, of course, they may confirm the assumptions. At any rate, a desire to substitute empirical data for subjective speculation in policy debates has led to increased research of this sort.[10]

Even though there still is a paucity of hard data on such matters, there is good reason to believe that misconceptions about delinquency are widespread; if this is true, social scientists will have a special responsibility to inform the public of the current knowledge in this area. Some of the more likely misconceptions reflect general views on crime and punishment, rather than on youthful crime or misconduct. Hence, the tendency towards "compartmentalizing crime" applies to delinquency as well as to adult offenses.[11] We often prefer to see crime and delinquency as alien phenomena, as somehow existing *outside of* society, involving attacks *on* society. These disturbing acts, we would like to think, do not reflect the normal workings of our social system, but rather represent some kind of aberrational malfunctioning of the system. Were it true, such an idea might well be reassuring, but clearly it is not. Crime and delinquency, along with other problems, are integral features of our social order and hence cannot be explained by reference to some "external" or "abnormal" phenomena or occurrences. Unfortunately, the persisting unwillingness to face up to this fact (and the related fact that legislation itself "produces" crime and delinquency) has even led some sociologists to commit what they term the "evil causes evil" fallacy. This fallacy, that "bad" consequences must have "bad" causes, blinds one to the ways in which socially disturbing behavior may be grounded in aspects of the dominant social structure and prevailing value systems.

A corollary of this reasoning is the belief that such problems as crime and delinquency always require *special* solutions. Failure to appreciate the complex interrelationships between diverse aspects of the social system (including these allegedly offensive ones) narrows the vision of those who would seek to induce change. One particularly unfortunate result of this is an inordinate focus on the individual deviants or "offenders" themselves. Such individuals are seen as being *basically* different from the nonoffenders (that is, quite apart from the mere difference of engaging in norm violations), and it is in this basic differentness that the "causes" of delinquency problems are believed to lie. (As can readily be seen, this view is part and parcel of the belief that delinquency is a real entity and is sharply distinguished from normal conduct.) The various approaches professionals have taken in analyzing the causes of delinquency reveal that their orientations differ considerably in the extent to which they accept or incorporate this "differentness" theme. Although this theme carries a great appeal (perhaps because it helps some of us convince ourselves we are basically and totally "good" or "normal"), it finds little support in the growing body of data concerning the nature and social distribution of youthful misconduct and delinquent "careers."

A more specific kind of misconception has to do with the social contexts of delinquency and the nature of delinquent acts. In this case, the distortion may be attributable largely to selective emphases by the mass media. Gang violence is probably the dominant image of delinquency carried by the media. This is misleading in several respects. To begin with, although it is undoubtedly true that much youthful law violation is done by groups, the term "gang" has been used in highly variable and often questionable ways. As a close student of gang behavior recently noted, both the media and official criminal justice agencies may use the term too casually:

> Depending on the context, the reporter's viewpoint, and the current predispositions of his editor, a slight melee at a rock-and-roll festival or a "love-in" may be described as youthful exuberance, political protest, or gang hooliganism. When the Los Angeles Police Department maintained a gang intelligence squad during the early 1960s, a gang incident was defined *as any legal infraction involving three or more juveniles,* and a gang was *any group of eight or more juveniles.* For most purposes, such arbitrary criteria are patently useless and misleading, yet for police intelligence purposes they served what seemed to be necessary functions for maintaining records and "selling" the notion of widespread incidence of gang delinquency.[12]

The same commentator pointed out that the vagueness of professionals sometimes has exacerbated this confusion: "We slip back and forth in our thinking among subculture, reference group, and membership group; between primary and secondary group; among groups, gangs, companions, and legal co-subjects." [13]

Not only has the term "gang" been used too loosely, but the media also have conveyed the impression especially that gang violence is the dominant form of delinquency. Yet various researchers have pointed out that this is just not so. Miller found, for example, in his Boston studies that "Acts of theft were two to three times as common as acts of assault, the next most frequent type of offense." [14] Similarly—Klein, reporting on research in Los Angeles, noted that thefts, juvenile status offenses (truancy, incorrigibility, and so on), and auto theft were all more frequent than assaultive acts—the first being by far the most common offense. Newspaper coverage during the same period, however, concentrated almost exclusively on violent crimes against persons.[15] As Miller suggests, regarding "this preoccupation with relatively uncommon forms of youth crime at the expense of its most common form," emotional reactions to particular kinds of crime seem to have warped perceptions: "Violent crimes by youth—gang fights, gang assaults on individuals, sexual attacks—have particular power to evoke feelings of fear, threat, and danger among adults." [16] A similar tendency for the general public to disproportionately notice violence among adult offenses has been cited by the President's crime commission and various other observers.

DELINQUENCY TYPOLOGIES

How is one to make sense of the myriad research findings and theories about delinquency? Efforts to bring greater coherence to this field often have led to the construction of typologies—classificatory schemes designed to break down and organize the data of delinquency in a theoretically meaningful way. Unfortunately these efforts, at least when viewed collectively, have been less than fully successful. As Ferdinand comments:

> Out of all this interest in typologies, however, a precise delimitation of the types of delinquents or criminals that exist has *not* been forthcoming. Instead of the hoped-for convergence, we find typologies based upon legal categories, typologies drawn from psychoanalytic theory, typologies based upon sociological theory and physiological factors, and typologies derived impressionistically from empirical data. Each of these attempts to capture the essence of crime or delinquency is certainly valid in its own right, but taken together they do *not* provide a progressively finer analysis of deviant behavior. Instead, they present us with a patchwork of typologies that are either incomparable or contradictory.[17]

From a sociological standpoint, and for reasons to be considered more fully in the next chapter, the least successful of the typologies are those that classify the *kinds of persons* involved in delinquency. As one might expect, the prototype of such efforts is the psychodynamic classification aimed at diagnosis. But as we shall see, some sociologists have also built their typologies (and their theories) around the "kinds of persons" issue. The basic difficulty with such typologies has already been alluded to: they are usually grounded on the assumption that *special* kinds of people are involved in delinquency. Many sophisticated sociological observers now believe that such an assumption is largely unwarranted, not only with respect to deeply ingrained personality characteristics or patterns, but even with respect to social background. The latter, especially, is a thorny issue in delinquency research, and we shall return to it later.

The bases for classifying individuals are usually governed by the professional orientations of the researchers. Not too surprisingly, psychologists produce psychological typologies, sociologists produce sociological ones. This has led to the criticism that such typologies arbitrarily consider separate factors and processes that in fact work in combination to "produce" delinquency, and that some greater effort at synthesis is required:

> . . . assuming that delinquency is influenced both by psychological and social forces, a synthetic typology of delinquency would describe the behavior of individuals with typical personality styles in typical social situations. By examining systematically the personality types that psychological theory suggests in terms of certain common social situations, it should be possible to construct a synthetic typology that coordinates the insights of both points of view in the explanation of delinquency.[18]

Unfortunately no analyst has yet produced a synthetic typology of this sort on which substantial cross-disciplinary agreement could be reached. In part this is due to professional ethnocentrism, but at the same time it reflects the extreme complexity of the task; it is even possible that contradictory assumptions and goals (discussed below) render such an attempt untenable.

Martin, Fitzpatrick, and Gould (two sociologists and a psychiatrist), in a recent study (not, however, primarily concerned with typology development) have made an ambitious effort to bring diverse professional orientations to bear in field research on delinquency. Asserting that "the meaning of an act which the dominant society terms delinquent can be adequately understood only when the full range of social, cultural, situational, *and* personal variables involved have been identified and related to one another," they call for research utilizing three orientations: the "sociogenic case history," which places the individual culturally, socially, and institutionally, and also covers personality variables; "situational analysis," which focuses on the situations within which delinquent acts occur, including the reactions of others to the individual's behavior; and "area analysis (or epidemiological) method," which examines demographic aspects of the problem.[19] However, it is much easier to *identify* the full range of variables that *may* be involved in delinquency (and the authors are more successful at this) than to demonstrate *how* the variables are interrelated, and which ones are most central in causing delinquency. So-called "synthetic" formulations and typologies (to adopt Ferdinand's term) sometimes degenerate into injunctions to examine anything and everything that might be relevant to delinquency. Thus while Martin, Fitzpatrick, and Gould wisely recognize that delinquency involves much more than special "kinds of people," their work also suggests the formidable difficulties of integrating the study of individuals with a broader sociocultural analysis of delinquency problems.

Another sort of typology that still represents a classification of individuals but is not simply a "kinds of people" categorization, is organized around the notion of offender types. Gibbons, describing offender patterns in terms of offense behavior, interactional setting, self-concept, and attitudes, delineates nine major delinquent role types:

> Predatory gang delinquent
> Conflict gang delinquent
> Casual gang delinquent
> Casual delinquent, nongang member
> Automobile thief ("joyrider")
> Drug user (heroin)
> Overly aggressive delinquent
> Female delinquent
> "Behavior problem" delinquent[20]

For each type, Gibbons discusses typical social class and family backgrounds, peer-group associations, and contact with "defining agencies." These are broad and necessarily rather superficial portraits, and as Gibbons himself notes elsewhere, there is always something arbitrary about such classifications:

. . . typological schemes put more order into juvenile lawbreaking than exists in fact. For one thing, we need to remember that delinquents are juveniles, not full-blown adults. They are relatively unsophisticated individuals; many of them are uninformed on the ways of criminality. . . . Their interests fluctuate, so that we should be surprised if many of them have made strong commitments to particular forms of lawbreaking. Then, too, the vicissitudes of police-offender interaction, court appearance, and the like are such that many of them are able to drift in and out of misconduct. For all of these reasons, clear-cut careers of specialized delinquency are probably uncommon.[21]

Nonetheless, a typology that is centered around offense behavior may have special usefulness in formulating delinquency policies and programs. Such a typology helps us to recognize that it is not just one type of individual who engages in delinquent acts; and similarly, that no single "treatment" program (a major concern in Gibbons's work) will be equally appropriate to all the diverse patterns of individual background, social situation, and official reaction involved in the various offenses. We shall return to the topic of treatment in the next chapter. But to cite just a few examples, as Gibbons notes, special needs for "affectional relationship" appear to characterize many female delinquents; presumably, this calls for a particular type of treatment. Likewise, while the situation of heavy drug users may call for a residential drug-free treatment program along the lines of the Synanon model, something quite different may be appropriate in dealing with street gangs. Finally, breaking delinquency down into offense categories may help us to keep in mind broader policy issues, including the question of whether particular types of behavior should be considered "delinquent" in the first place.

Whereas the typologies considered so far attempt to order the empirical data of delinquency, a related effort seeks to classify the *theories* about delinquency. The most common and least useful classification of theories is "psychogenic" and "sociogenic," with perhaps an "integrated" theory category. Some of the shortcomings of such an approach already have been suggested. As we shall see, something other than its psychological or sociological emphasis often distinguishes a delinquency theory; hence, to classify theories in this manner may prove unilluminating. Sociologists have sought to develop more refined classifications of theories (usually concentrating on the sociological work, but often using rubrics that cut across disciplinary lines), designating them as "anomie theory," "cultural transmission theory," "interaction process theory," and the like.[22] In a recent and important work, Hirschi specifies three major categories of delinquency theory:

> According to *strain* or motivational theories, legitimate desires that conformity cannot satisfy force a person into deviance. According to *control* or bond theories, a person is free to commit delinquent acts because his ties to the conventional order have somehow been broken. According to *cultural deviance* theories, the deviant conforms to a set of standards not accepted by a larger or more powerful society.[23]

Unfortunately, there is considerable lack of agreement as to what the major categories are (and just how they should be designated), and to a lesser extent there is disagreement on the proper placement of the more specific formulations within any given set of categories.

However, classifying theories of delinquency may enable us to organize the diverse findings from empirical research so that we can make some theoretical generalizations. Often the empirical findings indicate only that some factor or other is significant in causing delinquency. A theoretical formulation must relate this finding to others and specify how these factors lead to delinquency. As Martin and Fitzpatrick point out, referring to the numerous associations found through research between delinquency and such factors as poverty, slum residence, dropping out of school, and the like: "Nothing about such factors, or about hundreds of others that could be listed, helps to explain delinquency unless such factors are treated as variables, which are then tied together logically and given meaning in terms of some process that leads to delinquency. Specification of such a process is what constitutes a theory of delinquency causation." [24] Theory, for the social scientist, is not separate from fact; it is simply a way of organizing and interpreting the facts.

A NEW APPROACH

Much work in the sociology of delinquency, particularly when it involves a high level of theorizing, seems remote from the realities of delinquent behavior and the problems of dealing with it in the real world. Not only is it difficult for the concerned citizen to comprehend what the sociologist is trying to accomplish with his table-mongering and word-spinning, but also one can easily feel that these activities in no way impinge on the actual delinquency policies and programs. In other words, it could be argued that the theories make no real difference.

This is simply not the case. On the contrary, there is a complex interaction process linking delinquency problems, policies, research, and theory. It is entirely too glib to assume that policies represent a direct, "pure" response to evident problems, and that research and theory-construction on the other hand arise only out of the strictly scientific objectives and interests of the social scientist. More typically, policy responses are mediated through a body of understanding about the problematic behavior or conditions, understanding that rests in part on the knowledge social scientists have accumulated and in part on ideological and other bases. Social science knowledge of delinquency is, after all, formally transmitted to many practitioners in the delinquency field as part of their professional training; and although "on-the-job socialization" is as important to the field worker as his formal education, it is unlikely that the latter has no impact. It is significant that in the survey of the California Youth Authority staff cited earlier almost half the respondents listed specific behavioral scientists whose work had influenced their understanding of delinquency (in this instance, psychologists and psychiatrists outnumbering sociologists).[25] Nor are legislators or even the general public immune to the impact of social science. Increased reliance by governmental commissions on the advisory and staff work of social science specialists, the growing prestige of the social science disciplines, and the related popularization of many social science terms and ideas all point in this direction.

At the same time, the student of delinquency is not immune to extrascientific influences. His research and theorizing often reflect his "gut reactions" to particular social problems, his ideological predispositions, the influence of policy-makers and others on whom he may have to rely for support, and his professional vested interests. Furthermore, his core assumptions about human behavior, his preferences in research methodology, and the influence of more general theoretical developments in his discipline (and, in this instance, particularly the elaboration of general theories of deviance and social control) may also shape his delinquency studies.

This study is concerned with *patterned reactions* to delinquency. The reactions in this area are not idiosyncratic, and those of the public, practitioners, and social scientists are not unrelated. The sociologist's greatest contribution to our understanding of delinquency problems may lie not in accumulating empirical data about delinquent offenses and offenders, nor even in developing "causal" theories in the technical sense, but rather in helping us to understand why we have reacted to the problems we have called "delinquency" in particular ways and what the consequences of those reactions have been.

Major categories of reaction to be discussed in the chapters that follow are shown in Table 1. These patterns—individual treatment, liberal reform, and radical nonintervention reactions—do not represent the only possible responses to delinquency. One response that is not treated at length here, and with which we are all familiar, is the get-tough antipermissive approach to crime and delinquency problems. Conservative politicians and some law-enforcement officials often express this outlook, insisting that wrongdoers must be dealt with sternly and that misconduct "will not be tolerated." Although the roots of this reaction may run deep in the human psyche, and may also reflect the powerful "good guys, bad guys" theme in American culture, this response—at least in its most blatant forms —does not at present exert a significant influence on delinquency policies. At the same time, and as the discussion below may suggest,

TABLE 1. REACTIONS TO DELINQUENCY

	INDIVIDUAL TREATMENT	LIBERAL REFORM	RADICAL NONINTERVENTION
Basic assumptions	Differentness of offenders delinquency a symptom; psychosocial determinism	Delinquency concentrated in lower class; individual constrained— particularly by subcultural pressures; social determinism	Delinquency wide-spread through-out society; basic role of contingencies; neo-antidetermin-ism
Favored methodologies	Clinical; comparison of matched samples	Analysis of rate variations; ecological analysis; study of subcultures	Self-reports; observation; legal analysis
Focal point for research	The individual	Social class; local community	Interaction be-tween the indi-vidual and the legal system (and other agencies of reaction)
Representa-tive causal perspectives	Psychodynamic theories; family-oriented theories;	Anomie theories; cultural transmission; opportunity theory	Labeling analysis; drift and situa-tional theories
Prevention	Identification of "predelin-quents"; probation and counselling	Street gang work; community pro-grams; piecemeal socio-economic re-form	Deemphasis on singling out specific indi-viduals; radical socio-cultural change
Treatment	Therapy; training schools	Community pro-grams; improving condi-tions in institu-tions	Voluntary treat-ment
Juvenile court	"Individualized justice"; rehabilitative ideal	Better training and caseloads; more attention to social factors	Narrow scope of juvenile court jurisdiction; increased formalization

many observers believe that feelings of this sort do represent an important covert influence lying behind many ostensibly "lenient" attitudes and policy measures. Thus the authors of a recent work on schools and delinquency write of our present obsession with law and order and claim that, "One manifestation of this obsession is the development of what amounts to a virtual war on youth. Prompted by civil-rights activism, increasingly violent student protests, and the challenge of traditional standards of morality as reflected in sexual behavior and drugs, society is creating and utilizing increasingly punitive legal mechanisms to control youthful misbehavior." [26] Similarly Platt, in the conclusion to his fascinating sociohistorical analysis of the juvenile justice movement, asserts:

> With the rise of black militancy in recent years, there has been a corresponding hardening of official antidelinquency programs. Intelligence units are supplementing and sometimes replacing youth officers, and police have developed counterinsurgency techniques to manage gangs. Self-help efforts by urban youth are generally discredited, and "youth programs" rarely involve young people in the decision-making process. Rather than increasing opportunities for the exercise of legitimate power by adolescents, public agencies have opted for closer supervision as a means of decreasing opportunities for the exercise of illegitimate power.[27]

Although this seems an excessively sombre assessment of overall trends, nonetheless anti-youth sentiments have a strong potential influence.

The most influential ways of viewing delinquency, however, coalesce around the three major reaction patterns depicted in Table 1. What exactly do these patterns represent? To begin with, they are what the sociologist calls "ideal types." They are built up to some extent on a base of empirical data, but more crucially, they are constructed through a process of theoretical and logical elaboration of assumptions, interconnections, and implications. These are, then, broadly formulated depictions of three basic ways of looking at delinquency. As the analysis that follows should make clear, they are not merely hypothetical constructs. On the other hand (and this is one of the central meanings of sociological ideal types generally), rarely if ever do they appear in pure form. We are unlikely to find individuals who react to delinquency in terms of every single ideal characteristic of, say, the treatment reaction, and nothing more. Most persons' responses do, however, organize themselves around one or another of these models. And this is not necessarily because they have carefully thought through all aspects of the problem. Rather, it occurs because each pattern is grounded in certain core assumptions and basic outlooks that in turn imply a whole complex of interrelated preferences.

This aspect of cognitive and logical interrelatedness in part provides the basis for an unusual feature of the typology presented here —namely that it incorporates both types of causation theory and research, on the one hand, and types of public policy on the other. A strong strain to consistency usually will make those who hold particular basic assumptions about delinquency select research procedures and public policies that are also characteristic of the basic response pattern.

The categories, however, are not mutually exclusive. While in some respects the reaction patterns will be contradictory or inconsistent, in others they will be compatible or even complementary (although compatibilities are more likely to be found between the individual treatment and liberal reform patterns than between either of those and the radical nonintervention pattern). Most delinquency research and policy has reflected the combined influence of the first two orientations, and the line between them is actually rather hazy. Whereas the treatment reaction places great stress on the distinctive characteristics of individual "offenders," the liberal reform response focuses on the social class and subculture of delinquency. Yet some of the more sophisticated methods for "treating" individuals clearly take socioeconomic status and cultural context into account, and practitioners who use these methods may well hold "liberal reform" assumptions. Similarly, efforts to control delinquency through the community and "street" activities that reform premises dictate cannot avoid dealing with (if not formally "treating") individuals. Furthermore, certain critics of liberal reform have suggested that basic assumptions of the treatment model (particularly the differentness, even the blameworthiness, of the "offender") continue to lurk behind policies supposedly concerned with more general social reform. The distinction between treatment-reform policies and the radical nonintervention reaction is more clear-cut.

In radical nonintervention delinquents are seen not as having special personal characteristics, nor even as being subject to socio-economic constraints, but rather as *suffering from contingencies.* Youthful "misconduct," it is argued, is extremely common; delinquents are those youths who, for a variety of reasons, drift into disapproved forms of behavior and are caught and "processed." A great deal of the labeling of delinquents is socially unnecessary and counterproductive. Policies should be adopted, therefore, that accept a greater diversity in youth behavior; special delinquency laws should be exceedingly narrow in scope or else abolished completely, along with preventive efforts that single out specific individuals and programs that employ "compulsory treatment." For those serious offenses that cannot simply be defined away through a greater tolerance of diversity, this reaction pattern may paradoxically increase "criminalization"—uniformly applied punishment not disguised as treatment; increased formalization of whatever juvenile court procedures remain, in order to limit sanctioning to cases where actual antisocial acts have been committed and to provide constitutional safeguards for those proceeded against.

While this mode of responding to delinquency problems departs sharply from earlier reactions, even this "radical" outlook has some ties to the other approaches. This is particularly true of the reform reaction. Although the nonintervention response does not view socioeconomic reform as *the* solution to delinquency problems, most of its proponents would favor a radical change of major institutions and prevailing cultural values. Not all forms of individual treatment, however, are anathema to those espousing the nonintervention response. The crucial objection is to *compulsion;* even "therapy"—while it does not provide a major solution to delinquency problems—is quite compatible, provided the individual submits to it voluntarily.

Similarly, the noninterventionists were hardly the first persons to favor narrowing the juvenile court jurisdiction and formalizing the court's procedures. In some respects the three major reaction patterns reflect a chronological and cumulative development in delinquency research and policy-making. Nevertheless, there are still those today who insist on narrow modes of individual treatment and those who concentrate exclusively on the individual characteristics of "offenders." However, work in delinquency has to a large extent progressed from a narrow emphasis on the offending individual, through an increased attention to sociocultural context, and on to the nonintervention focus on patterns of interaction between "deviants" and social control agents. At each stage, certain aspects of the former approach have been discarded, while others have been retained for their usefulness.

✠ ✠ ✠

1. Anthony M. Platt, *The Child Savers: The Invention of Delinquency* (Chicago: University of Chicago Press, 1969), p. 4.

2. Doug Knight, *Delinquency Causes and Remedies: The Working Assumptions of California Youth Authority Staff* (Sacramento: California Youth Authority, February, 1972), p. x.

3. *In Re: Gault*, 387 U.S. 1 (1967).

4. Don C. Gibbons, *Delinquent Behavior* (Englewood Cliffs, N.J.: Prentice-Hall, Inc., 1970), p. 7.

5. President's Commission on Law Enforcement and Administration of Justice, *Task Force Report: Juvenile Delinquency and Youth Crime* (Washington, D.C.: U.S. Government Printing Office, 1967), p. 25.

6. Edwin M. Schur, *Our Criminal Society: The Social and Legal Sources of Crime in America* (Englewood Cliffs, N.J.: Prentice-Hall, Inc., 1969), p. 2.

7. See Edwin M. Schur, *Law and Society: A Sociological View* (New York: Random House, Inc., 1968), especially pp. 5–8.

8. Hermann Mannheim, *Criminal Justice and Social Reconstruction* (New York: Oxford University Press, 1946), p. 1.

9. Francis A. Allen, *The Borderland of Criminal Justice* (Chicago: University of Chicago Press, 1964), p. 31.

10. For example, see President's Commission on Law Enforcement and Administration of Justice, *Task Force Report: Assessment of Crime* (Washington, D.C.: U.S. Government Printing Office, 1967), pp. 85–95; reprinted in Paul Lerman, ed., *Delinquency and Social Policy* (New York: Frederick A. Praeger, Inc., 1970), pp. 358–77; also Julius Cohen, Reginald A. H. Robson, and Alan Bates, *Parental Authority: The Community*

and the Law (New Brunswick, N.J.: Rutgers University Press, 1958); Arnold M. Rose and Arthur Prell, "Does the Punishment Fit the Crime? A Study in Social Valuation," *American Journal of Sociology*, 61 (November, 1955), 247–59; and Elizabeth A. Rooney and Don C. Gibbons, "Social Reactions to 'Crimes Without Victims,'" *Social Problems*, 13 (Spring, 1966), 400–410.

The growing theoretical emphasis on societal reactions to deviance is seen in John Kitsuse, "Societal Reaction to Deviance: Problems of Theory and Method," *Social Problems*, 9 (Winter, 1962), pp. 249–56; and J. L. Simmons, "Public Stereotypes of Deviants," *Social Problems*, 13 (Fall, 1965), 223–32.

11. Schur, *Our Criminal Society*, pp. 9–12.

12. Malcolm W. Klein, *Street Gangs and Street Workers* (Englewood Cliffs, N.J.: Prentice-Hall, Inc., 1971), pp. 7–8.

13. *Ibid.*, p. 12.

14. Walter B. Miller, "Theft Behavior in City Gangs," in Malcolm W. Klein, ed., *Juvenile Gangs in Context* (Englewood Cliffs, N.J.: Prentice-Hall, Inc., 1967), p. 28.

15. Klein, *Street Gangs and Street Workers*, pp. 16–17.

16. Miller, "Theft Behavior," p. 29.

17. Theodore N. Ferdinand, *Typologies of Delinquency: A Critical Analysis* (New York: Random House, Inc., 1966), p. 41.

18. *Ibid.*, p. 55.

19. John M. Martin, Joseph P. Fitzpatrick, and Robert E. Gould, *The Analysis of Delinquent Behavior: A Structural Approach* (New York: Random House, Inc., 1970), pp. 15–20.

20. Don C. Gibbons, *Changing the Lawbreaker* (Englewood Cliffs, N.J.: Prentice-Hall, Inc., 1965), Ch. 3.

21. Gibbons, *Delinquent Behavior*, p. 96.

22. For an extremely useful discussion along these lines, see Albert K. Cohen, *Deviance and Control* (Englewood Cliffs, N.J.: Prentice-Hall, Inc., 1966).

23. Travis Hirschi, *Causes of Delinquency* (Berkeley: University of California Press, 1969, 1970), p. 3.

24. Martin, Fitzpatrick and Gould, *Analysis of Delinquent Behavior*, p. 155.

25. Knight, *Delinquency Causes and Remedies*, p. 115.

26. Kenneth Polk and Walter E. Schafer, eds., *Schools and Delinquency* (Englewood Cliffs, N.J.: Prentice-Hall, Inc., 1972), p. 7.

27. Platt, *Child Savers*, pp. 179–80.

TREATING THE INDIVIDUAL

The treatment reaction is grounded in the *assumption of basic differentness*. Delinquency, in this view, is attributable primarily to the special characteristics of individual delinquents; and indeed those who adopt this outlook are more likely than others to accept the notion that "delinquent" is a useful and empirically meaningful term. To understand delinquency, we must pursue research aimed at ferreting out the delinquent's unique characteristics —accumulating data about individual offenders through in-depth clinical observation and analysis, or through statistical comparison of "matched" samples of delinquents and nondelinquents. Similarly, efforts to deal with delinquency problems must center on the problems of these offending individuals. Basically, the treatment response asserts: we have delinquency because we have delinquents; we must do something *to* or *for* them if we are to rid ourselves of the problem.

29

In a most insightful discussion of this orientation, Matza notes that its basic assumptions as well as the research and policy preferences its adherents adopt, clearly reflect the legacy of "positive criminology" that began with Lombroso and that has continued to wield a considerable influence. For the positivists the important thing, if criminology were to become a science, was to shift attention from the crime to the criminal.

> Differentiation is the favored method of positivist explanation. Each school of positive criminology has pursued its own theory of differentiation between conventional and criminal persons. . . . A reliance on differentiation, whether constitutional, personal, or sociocultural, as the key explanation of delinquency has pushed the standard-bearers of diverse theories to posit what have almost always turned out to be empirically undemonstrable differences.[1]

As Matza goes on to make clear, the common ground for these diverse attempts at criminological differentiation (engaged in by sociologists as well as psychologists and psychiatrists), lay in the notion of *constraint*. "Determinism for the positive school of criminology was not merely a heuristic principle; it was a vision that likened man to physical and chemical particles. Every event is caused. Human freedom is illusory."

Furthermore, not only did this "hard determinism" seem to help the social sciences to become like the natural sciences, but it also supported humanitarian reforms: "The negation of freedom not only suited the pretensions and ambitions of social science; it also was a fundamental requirement of a view that commended the treatment of criminals. Persons without choice are not responsible for their actions. Instead of punishment, they require treatment or other forms of correction." [2] Certainly the versions of constraint posited under the individual treatment and the liberal reform reactions differ, and to that extent the logical policy implications under the two models also differ; but both responses rest on the general notion that man's behavior is strongly determined, that there are powerful forces (whether "internal" or "external") that push the individual toward particular actions.

These prevalent assumptions of differentiation (between offenders and nonoffenders) and determinism explain why critics often contend that an inappropriate "medical model" or "medical analogy" has governed much of the work on delinquency. Delinquent acts have usually been viewed as symptomatic of an underlying disorder. Sometimes that disorder has been seen to lie in the individual himself, at other times in the social system. In either case, this notion has an important implication for research and policy: namely, that one must understand and treat the underlying condition and not merely its symptoms. Needless to say, particular treatment philosophies vary tremendously. The more sociologically oriented ones, taking into account the importance of situational factors, may emphasize particular *forms* of delinquency. Yet the treatment outlook and to a lesser extent the reform outlook (insofar as it incorporates treatment premises) imply that persons with certain characteristics (psychological or social) will be relatively *predisposed* to engage in delinquent behavior, whatever specific forms this may take.

THEORIES AND METHODS

Etiological theories most characteristic of the individual treatment reaction assert innate, or "internal," causes of delinquency. The assumptions of differentiation and determinism would best be substantiated if they could be supported by constitutional, and preferably hereditary, factors that distinguish delinquent offenders. However, as Gibbons succinctly states:

> The plain fact is that many years of biogenic exploration of delinquency have not yielded any valid generalizations about biological factors in deviance. Almost without exception, the biological theories that have been advanced have been scientifically naïve, while the research that has been conducted has been flawed in one way or another. Although it cannot unequivocally be claimed that there are no biogenic influences in delinquency, it is undeniably true that none have so far been shown to exist.[3]

BIOLOGICAL THEORIES. While the attempts of Lombroso to delineate physical "stigmata" by which one could identify the "born criminal," and the description of so-called "criminal families (as in the well-known studies of the Jukes and the Kallikaks) are no longer considered to be valuable contributions to an understanding of crime and delinquency,[4] biological explanations continue to have a hold on the public imagination. This approach permits those currently not in trouble with the law to set themselves apart from the "offenders," and to receive eagerly and accept uncritically every new constitutional theory that is offered.

To cite just one example, research findings presented at a recent meeting of specialists on learning disabilities, warranted a large-type six-column headline in the *New York Times* that read, "Experts Now Link a Learning Disorder to Delinquency."[5] According to this account, a neurological learning-disability syndrome, in which children of normal basic intelligence but with "a tiny physiological defect somewhere in the brain" are prevented from mastering basic learning skills, "is finally being recognized as a major cause of school failure, emotional disturbance, and even juvenile delinquency." The writer went on to refer to studies indicating that "as many as 80 percent of delinquent boys may have begun their downhill ride in society with a potentially correctable learning problem." No details of these studies were included in the article however, so the lay reader had absolutely no way of even tentatively evaluating the purported findings. It may well be true, of course, that such a condition contributes to the delinquent behavior of some youths. Indeed, the author's description of a typical developmental pattern accords with common sense and appears sociologically sound: "the child with a learning disability went through most of his schooling undiagnosed, was branded by others and himself as a failure and a troublemaker, left school as soon as he was legally allowed to, and never came anywhere near reaching his full intellectual potential."[6]

Immediately suspect in such an account, however, are the undisclosed research methods employed in reaching the "findings," and the implication that what is being presented is a general and widely applicable causal explanation. As we shall see, assertions of this sort are typically based on unrepresentative clinical data or methodology that is faulty in other respects. The sociologist will most strongly object to the unexplained reference to "as many as 80 percent of delinquent boys." This simply is not plausible—given what we know of the legal basis of delinquency, the variability of delinquent acts, the social forces and processes that generate much delinquency, the situational contexts within which it occurs, and the tentative and variable nature of many delinquent "careers." Factors such as these provide the grounds for objecting to most *kinds-of-people* explanations. Although it is perfectly conceivable that 80 percent of the children with this learning disability might become "delinquent," it is highly unlikely that 80 percent of delinquency would be attributable to this condition (which the article indicates afflicts approximately 3 percent of schoolchildren).

Perhaps the most influential recent statement asserting the relevance of constitutional factors to delinquency is that of the Gluecks, who found that mesomorphy (or athletic, muscular body type) was more predominant among the institutionalized delinquents they studied than among the nondelinquents.[7] The mesomorphy finding at once raises questions of interpretation, of the meaning, ordering, and interplay of variables, that plague formulations of basic characteristics of offenders. Demonstrating a statistical association between two variables does not provide a causal explanation. Both mesomorphy and delinquency might be attributable to a third "more basic" factor (in which case the apparent association between the two is spurious), or youths drawn into delinquency might somehow experience changes in their basic body type (in which case the causal ordering of the variables is faulty). At any rate, it is hard to see, from an isolated finding of this sort, just how body type may affect the developmental careers of young people in our society (the sociologist will insist that any such influence cannot be directly biological, but rather will involve effects of social interaction on the development of self-concepts), or how such a factor is related to delinquency. If the association between mesomorphy and delinquency is valid statistically, then, again, the relevant process is likely to be social rather than biological in nature. Gibbons suggests, for example, that by a process of social selection, "it is not unlikely that recruits to delinquent conduct are drawn from the group of more agile, physically fit boys. . . ."[8] Furthermore, the mesomorphy finding might be a result of the Gluecks' reliance on an institutionalized sample of adjudicated delinquents that obscures the responses of public officials, which operate as an "intervening variable." The point is succinctly drawn by Hirschi and Selvin: "Judges may see in a muscular, broad-shouldered boy more of a threat to the community than they see in his pale and skinny counterpart. If this is so, the differences in the proportions of mesomorphs among delinquent and nondelinquent populations could well stem from this attitude on the part of the judge." [9] This failure to consider official response as a possible intervening and explanatory variable has been a recurrent shortcoming of much causation research based on statistical comparisons.

PSYCHOLOGICAL THEORIES. Much more significant than biological theories, at least in their actual influence on public policies, have been the various psychological formulations on the causes of delinquency. "Various" is used because there is a multitude of specific psychological theories, no one of which would be subscribed to by anything close to all psychologists and psychiatrists working in this area. The considerable policy influence of the psychological approach seems due mostly to general features of the orientation and to the prestige and power of psychology and psychiatry in our society.

One concept that has been quite influential in earlier delinquency analysis—the psychopathic personality—uses both the biological and psychological explanations, and its association with the former may explain its decline from popularity. Two researchers who have surveyed the literature on psychopathy arrive at the following definition: "The psychopath is an asocial, aggressive, highly impulsive person, who feels little or no guilt and is unable to form lasting bonds of affection with other human beings." [10] Admitting that psychiatrists and neurologists have offered conflicting interpretations of this condition, the McCords find rejection in childhood to be a common element in many diagnoses of psychopathy. And they conclude that there seem to be three basic causal patterns:

Severe rejection, by itself, can cause psychopathy.

Mild rejection, in combination with damage to the brain area (possibly the hypothalamus) which normally inhibits behavior, causes psychopathy.

Mild rejection, in the absence of neural disorder, can result in psychopathy if certain other influences in the environment fail to provide alternatives.[11]

Although the fact that early lack of affection may lead to aggressive. antisocial behavior helps us to understand some instances of lawbreaking, sociological (and some psychiatric) critics of the psychopathy label have strong reservations about its casual and highly variable uses. Studies have shown, for example, that in roughly comparable prisons the diagnosis of inmates as psychopathic has varied from 5 percent to 98 percent, and that the literature on psychopathy is filled with endless numbers of highly varying types of behavior, traits, and characteristics allegedly linked to the disorder. Critics contend that "psychopathy" is a convenient term that the psychiatrist can apply to those individuals he is convinced are mentally disturbed but who do not fit the requirements of the more conventional diagnostic categories. This "wastebasket" term has been casually used to explain a variety of types of socially disapproved behavior—including drug addiction, various types of sexual behavior, and political extremism.

Typically, the clinician sees for diagnosis or treatment a "patient," about whose offending or problematic behavior he already has been made aware. If he tends to believe that anyone engaging in such behavior must, by definition, be disturbed, it becomes extremely difficult to distinguish between the offending acts themselves and the psychodynamic bases on which the acts are to be explained. This circularity was cogently noted by Lindesmith, in an early critique of psychiatric diagnoses of drug addicts. Referring to an unspoken assumption that "any trait which distinguishes addicts from nonaddicts is *ipso facto* a criterion of abnormality," Lindesmith went on to comment:

> Addicts are said to become addicted because they have feelings of frustration, lack of self-confidence, and need the drug to bolster themselves up. Lack of self-confidence is taken as a criterion of psychopathy or weakness. But another person becomes addicted, it is said, because of "curiosity" and a "willingness to try anything once," and this too is called abnormal. Thus, self-confidence and the lack of self-confidence are both signs of abnormal-

ity. The addict is evidently judged in advance. He is damned if
he is self-confident and he is damned if he is not." [12]

The McCords recognize that "much of the confusion arises from
viewing all deviant behavior as psychopathic. Many investigators,
particularly those who make unusually high estimates of the incidence of psychopathy, seem to use antisocial behavior as their
sole diagnostic criterion." Nonetheless, they assert, "most researchers
agree upon the existence of a distinct psychopathic syndrome." [13]

There have been efforts to develop more sociological explanations of the unsocialized persistent aggressive deviant,[14] and the
term "sociopath" now is used as frequently as "psychopath." Yet, for
a number of reasons already alluded to—including the fact that
aggressive acts comprise but a relatively small proportion of all delinquent behavior—there is little likelihood that even in its more
sociologized forms the concept will provide a major explanation of
delinquency. Furthermore, whatever terminology is employed, this
diagnosis is subject to prejudgment and circularity. Commenting on
an interesting research project, in which over 500 child-guidance
clinic patients and a smaller control group of nonpatients were
studied some thirty years later,[15] Gibbons concluded that although
much greater adult maladjustment was found among the patients
than among the controls, use of the concept of sociopathic personality to explain recurrent symptoms of maladjustment was not especially helpful:

> . . . no convincing evidence of this elusive disease appeared in
> this report. Instead, the argument looks tautological in form.
> While the report showed that many youngsters who get into
> juvenile courts and guidance clinics live fairly disordered lives
> as adults, making a career of failure, there was little evidence in
> this research that these individuals were pathological personali-
> ties. Indeed, some of the findings tended to undermine the socio-
> path concept. For example, the data suggested that those anti-
> social children who avoided the juvenile court or training school
> were less likely to become sociopaths than those who had been
> through these organizations.[16]

It is interesting that even those who use the concept of psychopathic personality—closely associated as it often has been with con-

stitutional factors—find it necessary to incorporate a sociocultural dimension in their analysis. The McCords, noting that "many criminals and delinquents, though socially maladjusted, are psychologically healthy people," suggest the need to distinguish between three basic types of offenders:

> The "socialized delinquent" who has, partly, been formed by a deviant subculture and who adheres to the values of his group
>
> The "neurotic delinquent," whose behavior springs from the anxiety created by unresolved, unconscious conflicts
>
> The "psychopathic delinquent" who commits a wide gamut of aggressive acts without anxiety, without guilt, and without attachment to any other human being[17]

A similar device, of specifying a category of "normals" for those offenders who do not display the psychopathological symptomatology on which the major diagnostic categories are premised, is evident in many of the psychoanalytic discussions of delinquency. This is so despite the fact that such discussions often are grounded in the belief that man's instincts or impulses are antisocial or asocial. According to an early and influential psychoanalytic treatment of crime, "within the innermost nucleus of the personality . . . it is impossible to differentiate normal from criminal impulses. The human being enters the world as a criminal, i.e., socially not adjusted." [18]

If orthodox psychoanalytic theory is particularly insistent on this basic criminality of man, and relies on a highly elaborated scheme of psychosexual development to explain early childhood influences, one way or another most psychological theories see delinquency as symptomatic of underlying psychodynamic or developmental disorders—whether the results are described in terms of inadequate superego development, weak ego strength, or other specialized concepts.

> As in biological theories, the specific factors determining delinquency are many and diffusely described. Delinquency results from an aggressive or antisocial personality arising out of parental

neglect, or perhaps overindulgence, or perhaps inconsistency; from a delinquent self-image arising out of criminal or delinquent role models, or perhaps an overbearing maternal figure who for reasons of her own encourages or discourages antisocial behavior; from specific neurotic syndromes—different delinquencies being manifestations of different neuroses; from the failure of parents to adequately socialize their children—delinquency being merely infantile, presocialized behavior; from an attenuation of the ego culminating in an inability to fathom the realistic consequences of transgression and an incapacity to resist the lure of companions.[19]

This dismaying compilation accurately depicts the vagueness of psychological thinking on delinquency. Certainly there have been advances over the years both in theoretical flexibility and methodological sophistication. The early theories that emphasize superego deficiencies (and the unconscious processes set in motion during the earliest childhood years),[20] have partly given way to an increased concern for ego processes and the continuing effects of social interaction and situational forces.[21] Then too, the more sophisticated psychiatric students of delinquency increasingly recognize that only some (and perhaps not even most) delinquent behavior is grounded in psychodynamic factors or requires psychotherapeutic treatment. Thus it may be recognized that the frequently encountered offender who, in terms of his own sociocultural milieu, is quite well socialized, rarely suffers from a psychological disorder.[22]

For the most part, however, the confusion of numerous theories remains, and the assumptions and procedures on which psychodynamic approaches to delinquency rest continue to reveal serious substantive and methodological weaknesses.[23] Sociological critics challenge not only the typical emphasis on early childhood and the assumption that youths in trouble somehow must be fundamentally different from those not in trouble, but more generally they point to many aspects of delinquency that most psychological explanations ignore. These aspects will often vary depending on the particular sociological emphasis of the critic, but typically will include the socioeconomic distribution of delinquent acts, group and other social contexts of delinquent behavior (including the existence of delinquent traditions in certain neighborhoods and subcultures), and the impact of official responses to initial acts of wrongdoing. With the growing emphasis in sociology on labeling and societal reactions, this last point becomes especially important.

Furthermore, the psychological delinquency theories provide an essentially *static* explanation of delinquent behavior, which is ironic given the interest of psychologists and psychiatrists in developmental process. However much these explanations may rest on asumptions regarding underlying processes, the processes themselves are brushed aside in the business of identifying the essential and initial differentness of delinquents. When the analyst posits the existence of a predisposition to delinquency,, "predelinquency," or "latent delinquency," he can then simply locate the condition in a young child and consider this sufficient to explain later wrongdoing. The processes by which an early state might lead to a later state— even assuming a valid relation between the two—is ignored. Indeed, it is as though time and experience stood still in the interim. This analytical jump, which presupposes that all the significant causal factors are operating during the early period, reflects a larger tendency in deviance theory (sociological as well as psychological) that Cohen has termed "the assumption of discontinuity." As he has noted, until recently "the dominant bias in American sociology has been toward formulating theory in terms of variables that describe initial states, on the one hand, and outcomes, on the other, rather than in terms of processes whereby acts and complex structures of action are built, elaborated, and transformed." [24] Becker, drawing a distinction between simultaneous and sequential models of deviance, similarly remarks: ". . . all causes do not operate at the same time, and we need a model which takes into account the fact that patterns of behavior *develop* in orderly sequence." [25]

Elsewhere Cohen has discussed the research strategies typically employed in static *kinds-of-people* comparisons, in which samples assumed to vary on an "independent variable" are examined to determine relative frequencies of deviant behavior. This mode of analysis, data from which usually are presented in fourfold tables, can be geared to sociological categories and factors (for example, socioeconomic background) as well as to psychological ones; indeed most delinquency studies involving statistical comparisons between presumed delinquents and nondelinquents follow this model. Even when the researcher takes "situational" factors into account, the tendency has been to develop comparisons while ignoring processes: "In these theories, if we are provided with certain data about the actor and certain data about the situation, the act is determined. There is, as it were, an abrupt move from a state of conformity to a state of deviance. The deviant act is like the reaction that occurs when we bring together two chemical substances." [26] When we consider (in Chapters Four and Five) the increasingly influential "labeling approach," we shall see that it uses an *interactionist* model in which human behavior is always viewed as developing through continuous and ever-changing processes of social interaction. A complete understanding of delinquency is only possible through an analysis that relates an individual's actions to the responses of others, including the very significant responses of official agents of social control.

It is not surprising, given these and other criticisms, that the psychodynamic work has not produced definitive findings on the distinctive personality characteristics of delinquents.[27] Some of the psychological analyses have been based solely on clinical data, without any comparison with nonpatient "control" subjects. Other studies have employed control groups, but have made naïve assumptions regarding the representativeness of samples of "delinquents" (usually individuals who have been adjudicated or institutionalized). As already noted, the psychologist or psychiatrist usually studies delinquents only after they have been adjudicated or otherwise officially identified. In such instances there is no way of determining whether any personality "findings" represent "causes" of the delinquency, or have developed as a consequence of the youth's involvement in delinquency; yet another alternative is that both the delinquency and the personality characteristics are attributable to some unknown third factor. Furthermore, since the individual's delinquency is known to the investigator, the dangers of circularity and prejudgment in diagnosis are very great.

Even some psychiatrists, criticizing their own profession, think that psychiatric concepts and practices have been overextended.

Szasz argues that most uses of the term "mental illness" involve an inappropriate application of medical analogy (since in his view most mental illness involves "problems in living" and hence is quite distinct from any organic illness).[28] The recourse to mental illness concepts to explain delinquency may carry an unwarranted analogy one step further. According to Szasz, "by seeking relief from the burden of his moral responsibilities, man mystifies and technicizes his problems in living. . . . The demand for 'help' thus generated is now met by a behavioral technology ready and willing to free man of his moral burdens by treating him as a sick patient." [29] We shall return later to this issue of responsibility, but it is worth reemphasizing here the powerful appeal of a supposed technical solution, particularly a medical one. If many Americans are quite prepared to cast aside openly moralistic judgments of wrongdoing, they may well be unable to accept the newer formulations (considered below) in which much delinquency is viewed as simply a reflection of the diverse behavior patterns of youth—neither bad as such, nor necessarily "sick." They would rather see "crime" as a form of "illness," whether this view rests on a firm scientific basis or not.

SOCIOLOGICAL APPROACHES. At the same time, it must be recognized that even with its many limitations the psychological approach has been trying to grapple with one important aspect of delinquency some other formulations tend to neglect; it confronts the basic question, Why did individual A engage in a delinquent act whereas individual B did not? Attempts to answer this question—which have tended heavily to take the form of *kinds-of-people* statistical comparisons—certainly are worthwhile, though they probably never can produce a comprehensive understanding of delinquency causation processes. It may be significant that even sociological analyses of delinquency, including some that proceed from assumptions quite different from those of the individual treatment reaction, are often thrown back on something like a psychological formulation to explain individual differences in behavior. Thus in ecological research, which analyzes the variations in delinquency rates between neighborhoods, census tracts, and other sections of a city, the researcher must also explain the fact of variation within these areas.

Depth analysis of the structural features of the city may explain why there are high-rate and low-rate areas, and hence may tell us a good deal about the causes of delinquency. Yet the fact remains that not all youths in the high-rate areas engage in delinquent acts, and likewise there are individual offenders within the low-rate areas. One major long-term sociological investigation of delinquency focused on this issue of "the good boy in the high-delinquency neighborhood." [30] Similarly, a leading study of juvenile drug use in urban areas, while finding an overwhelming concentration of drug users in those areas of New York characterized by the worst socioeconomic conditions, required a special hypothesis about differential family background factors to explain why only some residents of the high-rate areas took to drugs.[31]

Just as the ecological analyst finds he cannot ignore the individual delinquent, so too the investigator who seeks to explain delinquency by analyzing social class differences must sometimes use psychological concepts. As we shall see in the next chapter, there is an important body of sociological theory that attributes most delinquency to the strains and frustrations imposed on working-class youths by virtue of their low socioeconomic status. Even leaving aside the thorny point that many working-class youths never become officially recorded as delinquent, this thesis clearly fails to account for middle-class delinquency. To fill this gap in his version of the working-class strain theory, Cohen (drawing on earlier work by Parsons)[32] offers essentially a psychodynamic explanation of the delinquency of middle-class youth:

> Because of the structure of the modern family and the nature of our occupational system, children of both sexes tend to form early feminine identifications. The boy, however, unlike the girl, comes later under strong social pressure to establish his masculinity, his *difference from* female figures. Because his mother is the object of the feminine identification which he feels is the threat to his status as a male, he tends to react negativistically to those conduct norms which have been associated with mother and therefore have acquired feminine significance. Since mother has been the principal agent of indoctrination of "good," respectable behavior, "goodness" comes to symbolize femininity, and engaging in "bad" behavior acquires the function of denying his femininity and therefore asserting his masculinity.[33]

Cohen argues that the structural features involved, which Parsons saw as characteristic of the Western family generally, are intensified in the middle-class family situation. Since his major thesis about delinquency focuses on the social pressures facing working-class youths, perhaps it is not surprising that to explain the delinquent acts of middle-class youth (who do not confront such pressures), Cohen is drawn to an explantion that emphasizes individual motivation.

FAMILY INFLUENCES. A variety of other delinquency theories that point to family factors as having causal significance also reflect the assumptions of the individual treatment reaction pattern. One significant body of theory, emphasizing the family's role in strengthening personal and social "controls" that can insulate a youth from delinquency,[34] might at first glance seem tied to psychodynamic (early childhood) theories. Yet these formulations, in which there is currently renewed sociological interest, actually adopt a special stance on the issues of determinism and constraint that runs counter to the individual treatment response (as well as to the liberal reform response). For this reason, and because this stance fits in with other features of the radical nonintervention approach, it is considered more fully in Chapter Five, rather than here. Findings from the Gluecks' large-scale statistical study,[35] in which a constellation of family background factors (discipline of the father, supervision of the mother, affection of the father and the mother, and family cohesiveness) was held to be central in causing delinquency, reflect individual treatment assumptions and procedures. As we shall see in the next section, this study—employing statistical comparison of the characteristics of institutionalized delinquents and those of a sample of "matched" youths drawn from the noninstitutionalized population—has provided the basis for a highly controversial effort to predict potential delinquency early in childhood.

One might also place among the individual approaches all of the formulations that focus on the alleged influence of such factors as "working mothers" and "broken homes." There is a substantial literature documenting the deleterious effect on child development of extreme "maternal deprivation," [36] but it is unwarranted to claim that working mothers are "to blame" for delinquency. In a number of delinquency studies focusing on family factors, somewhat unclear and even partially contradictory findings have emerged on maternal employment.[37] Likewise, the simplistic assertions about "broken homes" that long have plagued this field are not fully corroborated by the available research findings. While there is little basis for ruling this factor out entirely as a relevant variable in delinquency causation, some studies suggest that it may have differential effects, depending on the age, sex, and area of residence of the child.[38]

Furthermore, most early studies on "broken homes" suffered from the methodological limitations inherent in the use of samples of adjudicated or institutionalized youths as representative of "delinquents." Thus, just as with the Gluecks' mesomorphy findings, official response may be a crucial intervening variable producing these outcomes. Hirschi and Selvin comment:

> . . . if attitudes of officials account for observed relations (or if analysts think they do), the search for intervening variables appears in a new light. Suppose that judges and other officials do react differently to children from broken homes and that this differential reaction accounts for the greater likelihood that a child from a broken home will be institutionalized. Insofar as this is true, the delinquency researcher will not be able to find a personality characteristic of the child that accounts for the relation between broken homes and delinquency. In other words, if attitudes of officials are responsible for associations between social characteristics and delinquency, then most quantitative studies of adjudicated delinquents, lacking data on the attitudes of officials, would be unable to demonstrate this.[39]

Even in attempts to deal with this methodological issue, where samples are drawn from the general population and delinquents determined on the basis of their self-reported behavior, one must be careful not to apply an unsophisticated mechanistic conception of the "broken home." The quality of relationships in the family, as seen in marital adjustment of the parents, affection between parents and children, and consistency and fairness of discipline, rather than its formal or external structure, appears to be the more important variable.[40]

We shall consider family-related variables with "absence of control" theories in a later chapter. In one sense, the family can be seen as an intervening variable in the processes by which one's position in the social class structure helps to determine the probability of involvement in delinquency. An important aspect of the family's influence concerns class differences in child-rearing practices.[41] However, family-related variables will not explain delinquency if we do not recognize their broader socioeconomic context. In drawing policy implications on the basis of their thorough review of the literature dealing with the family and delinquency, Rodman and Grams assert that "occupational deprivations underlie family instability and juvenile delinquency." And they go on to suggest:

> The key problem in the lower-class family is the weak occupational-economic position of the man. Since, in the United States, the man is expected to be the breadwinner above all else, he performs inadequately at his major role within the family. As a result the lower-class man is not esteemed, even within his own family, and he may be forced to play a peripheral position within his family. Under these circumstances, he may also leave his family. It can therefore be expected that improvements made in occupational and economic opportunities for lower-class men will strengthen their positiion within the family and thereby strengthen the stability of the family as a whole. It will also heighten the attractiveness of the father and the family in the eyes of the children and make additional resources available within the family. Such changes will make it possible for the family to maintain stronger controls over its children.[42]

Likewise, they see policies designed to provide equal opportunities for family planning and to educate parents on family problems (especially the impact of various child-rearing practices) as having an important potential in preventing delinquency. Whether or not such measures imply any latent bias (such as the desire of middle-class observers to view working-class families in their own image), family factors do not affect delinquency in a simple and direct way. The family is one vitally important factor in the youth's experience, but it is far from being the only one.

PREDICTING DELINQUENCY

One of the logical extensions of the individual treatment reaction is an interest in "early identification and intensive treatment" of delinquents. Unfortunately, as one close observer has noted, this is "more a slogan or a rallying cry than a realistic assessment of the difficulties that delinquency control programs must overcome." [43] It is understandable, however, that those adopting an individual-oriented outlook on delinquency persist in believing that it is possible (and desirable) to spot "predelinquents" before they get into serious difficulty, and to "nip in the bud" their antisocial behavior. Thus two commentators, who have done research involving one of the most popular of the delinquency-oriented personality tests—the Minnesota Multiphasic Personality Inventory—insist:

> . . . there is reason to believe that personality variables or patterns are related to the occurrence of delinquency in the sense of delinquency proneness. Some boys are so resistant to delinquent behavior that they will conform to social requirements under extremely difficult circumstances. By contrast, other boys will find ways to misbehave in good environments. Such observations make appropriate the acceptance of the construct "delinquency-proneness" manifested in the various rates of delinquency observed among children with various personalities living in a constant environment. Of course, no study can completely control the effect of environment, and all observed rates change as both personalities and environments vary. [44]

These same authors, not surprisingly, advocate viewing delinquency as symptomatic of an illness, and treating the underlying social and personal disorders that often lead to it. Toby, in his review of the literature in this area, is much less hopeful: "Whereas medical practice aims at precise diagnosis and specific treatment, early identification and intensive treatment of delinquency usually address themselves to an unknown problem with an unproved technique." [45]

The two best-known efforts at identifying predelinquency are the Cambridge-Somerville Youth Study,[46] and the New York City Youth

Board Study, which employed a prediction scale developed in the Gluecks' research.[47] The Cambridge-Somerville Study was based on what Toby calls "the principle of extrapolation"—in which the youths for whom delinquency is predicted are drawn from among those already seen as being in the early stages of troublemaking. Teachers, police, and others concerned with youth problems in the community were asked to provide names of boys who seemed headed for trouble. On the basis of these nominations and additional records, three judges (two social workers and a psychiatrist) made predictions regarding future delinquency. Some of these boys were given special intensive counseling (with disappointing results) while others were not; for the moment, our concern is with the prediction effort itself.

This study illustrates one of the most significant failings (and perhaps one of the greatest dangers) of prediction efforts—the tendency to overpredict delinquency. Follow-up some twenty years later of the predictions made in the Cambridge-Somerville study indicated that whereas approximately three-fifths of all cases had been considered predelinquent, less than one-third actually became involved with the law. One recent analysis of this finding notes that those making the predictions (the "judges") tended to assess how "difficult" the boy was in a very broad sense, rather than by a legalistic definition of delinquency:

> One judge said that for him a prediction of "difficult" signified an "incipient or actual antisocial career whether or not he [the boy] has come into open conflict with the law." For another, "difficult" referred to a disorganized personality; there was no explicit notion of conflict with the police and the courts. For the third, a "difficult" boy was one who "gets into difficulty with society," although he "may not be actually delinquent." [48]

These authors suggest that to test the accuracy of the predictions really would have required attention to more than formally designated delinquency or crime; that in terms of what they thought they were predicting the judges may not have greatly overpredicted.

However, many observers would say that the judges employed casual and overly broad notions of delinquency, and hence of "predelinquency." Gottfredson has recently insisted that delinquency predictions require scrupulous care and precision when specifying the criteria of delinquency; while a great deal of attention has been devoted to the issues surrounding predictor variables, there has been a tendency to assume glibly that we know precisely what it is we are trying to predict.[49] Particularly in the nonquantitative ("clinical," not "actuarial") prediction efforts, a combination of vagueness about delinquency criteria and casualness about predictor variables (i.e., indicators of "predelinquency") results in gross over-prediction. This danger may be exacerbated by loosely applying unsophisticated psychiatric assumptions. Thus, a sociological critic has noted that in one prevention project, the staff presented members of the community with a list of seventy different types of behavior or personality traits that might be considered symptoms calling for referral of children for diagnosis and treatment. The list included such contradictory qualities as "bashfulness" and "impudence," "bullying" and "dependence," "nailbiting" and "roughness" "overactivity" and "underactivity." Indeed, almost any childhood behavior would have seemed to permit a prediction of predelinquency in this particular scheme.[50]

Distinguishing between two types of prediction error, the "false positive" (an incorrect identification of an individual as likely to become delinquent) and the "false negative" (in which no later delinquency is predicted for an individual who in fact does become delinquent), Stanfield and Maher illuminate the dilemmas of prediction with an economic analysis:

> Each of these errors carries with it a cost. Some of this cost may be assessed in dollar terms. For example, if we know the cost of operating a delinquency-control program to be $200 per boy annually, then this is the annual cost of a false positive. On the other hand, if we also know that the cost of delinquent activity by one youth for one year runs to $5,000 then we know that one false negative costs as much as 25 false positives. Putting this argument in oversimplified terms, if 10 percent of the youths in a given community become delinquent, then the control program could be applied to all of them and still be less expensive than applying it to none of them, *provided that the control program effectively prevents delinquency in each case.*[51]

Unfortunately, as these authors note, the programs are not often effective, so it becomes necessary to include in the calculation the estimated cost of failures (based on past experience with the program). While such analyses may help introduce realism into policy-planning, critics insist that (as Stanfield and Maher themselves recognize) only some of the costs involved are financial. As we shall see in a moment, many observers feel that the possible human costs of false positive errors demand caution in carrying out programs based on predictive techniques.

The New York City Youth Board Study was grounded in what Toby terms the "principle of circumstantial vulnerability," according to which predelinquents are identified not by assessments based on their behavior to date, but rather by their exposure to circumstances believed likely to lead to delinquency. In this case, a predictive scale based on the five family factors (mentioned above) that the Gluecks found to be associated with delinquency was employed to assess probable delinquency among children aged 5½–6½ in certain high-delinquency areas of New York City. On the basis of a ten-year review of experience with this scale (and subsequently refined versions of it), spokesmen for the project claimed up to 85 percent accuracy in predicting eventual delinquency.[52] However critics have questioned the validity of these figures, raised questions about sampling procedures, and noted that predictions were more accurate for children in certain socioeconomic categories than for those in others.[53]

Furthermore, even if the claimed rate of predictive accuracy were correct, major problems of interpretation and implementation would remain. In one sense, if a predictive device works well enough, it is not necessary to know why it works. But if there is no theoretical understanding of the causation processes, there will be no meaningful framework for designing intervention efforts. (As a matter of fact, a school clinic program associated with the Youth Board Study did not effectively reduce delinquency among those predicted delinquents subjected to it.)[54] As methodological critics have emphasized, the Gluecks' findings were mostly presented in a great many two-variable tables; hardly any attempt was made to analytically determine genuine versus spurious relationships between variables, to validly establish the causal order of variables, or to examine the operation of possible intervening and explanatory variables.[55] It followed that the Youth Board, in making use of these findings, could not have any clear idea of the processes involved in delinquency causation; rather, they merely had at hand what seemed a convenient method for spotting eventual troublemakers. For this reason, Toby and other critics have questioned whether "an effective approach to delinquency control can emerge without clarification of the underlying intellectual issues in the etiology of delinquency." [56]

Quite apart from these and other essentially methodological problems,[57] major objections have been raised regarding the uses to which predictive devices may be put. Various commentators have emphasized that the term "individual prediction" is most misleading; these prediction techniques attempt to determine probable outcomes for different classes of cases. Some "false positive" errors are inevitable; if a given device predicts with an accuracy of 75 percent, then by definition it is going to be wrong 25 percent of the time. With this in mind, critics strongly object to singling out for special treatment children thus pinpointed. The core of this concern was well expressed by the Council of the Society for the Psychological Study of Social Issues in a statement issued in connection with a debate about the New York City Youth Board project:

> Unless the utmost caution and care are taken, children who are "identified" and labeled as probable future delinquents are likely to be treated and isolated as "bad" children by teachers and others who are now subjected to the virtually hysterical climate of opinion concerning juvenile delinquency. Such treatment is likely to increase the child's sense of social alienation and, thereby, increase the probability of his becoming delinquent or of developing other forms of psychological maladjustment.[58]

The renewed attention to labeling processes generally (discussed in Chapter Four) has heightened concern about such "boomerang" effects. What with the lack of demonstrated effectiveness in intervention programs, and the highly questionable assumptions underlying the prediction effort (especially the assumption that all essential "causal" factors have occurred at the time of prediction, and that no relevant processes will intervene between then and the time of tested outcome), it is not surprising that sociologists have evaluated these schemes quite negatively.

BEHAVIOR MODIFICATION

The logic of early identification leads to some rather severe forms of direct intervention in the lives of children. One of the most controversial involves the use of behavior-modifying drugs. According to Charles Witter, a former staff director of the Special Subcommittee on Invasion of Privacy of the U.S. House of Representatives, testimony before that body's hearings on this matter suggests that "200,000 children in the United States are now being given amphetamine and stimulant therapy, with probably another 100,000 receiving tranquilizers and antidepressants." He notes that "specialists in this therapeutic method state that at least 30 percent of ghetto children are candidates, and this figure could run as high as four to six million of the general grammar school population." [59] Witter goes on to point out that although such drugs do have some apparent short-term effectiveness in reducing hyperactive behavior and rendering inattentive and troublesome students more tractable, there has been very little systematic research on their long-range effects. Nevertheless, drug manufacturers have been extremely active in promoting the use of such drugs in the schools.

Critics assert that the drugs may indeed produce psychological or physiological harm in the children to whom they are administered.[60] Furthermore, they claim that the drugs are being used as an alternative to innovative teaching and sound educational planning, and also that they are being administered disproportionately to ghetto children. In a statement before the House Privacy Subcommittee, one leading educational specialist condemned the conditions prevailing in most urban schools (uninterested teachers who do not respect students, uninspired curriculum, severe discipline) and went on to say:

Then, when the children resist this brutalizing and stupefying treatment and retreat from it in anger, bewilderment, and terror, we say that they are sick with "complex and little-understood" disorders, and proceed to dose them with powerful drugs that are indeed complex and of whose long-term effects we know little or nothing, so that they may be more ready to do the asinine things the schools ask them to do.[61]

Several commentators indicate that since the predominantly white middle-class school personnel are quick to view nonwhite ghetto children as "difficult" or "nonresponsive," they are most likely to recommend drugs for them. Hentoff acknowledges having heard from parents who were enthusiastic about the effects of drugs given to their children, but he goes on to comment that *"without exception,* these have been middle-class parents who did not place their child in drug therapy until the child had been exhaustively diagnosed over a considerable period of time and through many different kinds of tests. And *without exception,* these middle-class kids have been carefully followed up while on medication. I can tell you flatly that this does not happen with the vast majority of poor kids on drugs in the public schools." [62]

Recently, governmental agencies concerned with crime control and corrections have shown considerable interest in a range of behavior-modification techniques that include "operant and classical conditioning, aversive suppression, and electronic monitoring and intervention." [63] These techniques vary tremendously in both the severity of the intervention involved and the degree of controversy they are likely to evoke. For example, under the heading of operant conditioning, Schwitzgebel describes two delinquency programs (one at the National Training School for Boys in Washington, D.C., the other a community-based program in Arizona) in which "reinforcers" such as points, marks, and privileges were successful in helping to promote desired behavior.[64] Such practices (like the "mark system," advocated long ago and from time to time used in adult corrections) do not involve intervention of a very controversial sort. However, and some might well find it a cause for alarm, directly following these descriptions the same writer refers to "operant conditioning of responses which have been traditionally associated with the autonomic nervous system." In various studies, "animals have been taught to increase or decrease heart rate, intestinal contractions, stomach contractions, urine formation, and electrical brain waves. Either direct electrical stimulation of the brain or escape from mild electrical shock has been used as a primary reinforcer. In some instances, clear and extreme physiological changes can be produced using this process." [65]

Schwitzgebel himself has advocated the use of various electronic techniques to deal with offenders in the community as an alternative to institutionalization. Thus he cites "the development, in prototype form, of small personally worn transmitters that permit the continual monitoring of the geographical location of parolees." [66] A related technique might involve devices worn by the individual that transmit signals to him (rather than the other way around)—possibly using electric shocks to deter him from undesired activity. Indeed, according to Schwitzgebel's account, "a new field of study may be emerging, variously known as behavioral engineering or behavioral instrumentation, that focuses upon the use of electro-mechanical devices for the modification of behavior." [67] Needless to say, the proponents of such techniques recognize that they raise constitutional and ethical issues. However, they argue that since such methods constitute treatment (Schwitzgebel at one point even uses the term "electronic rehabilitation") and may not only benefit the recipient but also provide an alternative to treatment in an institution, there are grounds for overruling typical objections (cruel and unusual punishment, invasion of privacy, and the like). But civil libertarians are not likely to be reassured by Schwitzgebel's comment regarding regulation of the practices: "Rather than relying upon case law or statutes, more flexibility and conceptual integrity could be obtained by having professional organizations and practitioners establish internal standards and guidelines. Courts and legislatures could then look to these standards in resolving difficult problems." Most observers undoubtedly would agree with him however, when he concludes that "The application of behavior modification techniques to the behavior of offenders necessarily involves some view of the relationship of the State's coercive power to the individual." [68]

COUNSELING, PROBATION, AND COMMUNITY TREATMENT

Most treatment policies tied to early identification efforts involve less severe and more commonly accepted modes of intervention than those envisioned in these behavior-modification schemes. One option that would seem particularly well adapted to the treatment orientation's premises is the intensive counseling of identified predelinquents. Unfortunately, as some comments above already have indicated, there is no consistent evidence for this technique's effectiveness. As mentioned, for example, the intensive counseling arranged by both the Cambridge-Somerville Youth Study and the New York City Youth Board Study failed to show a marked effect in reducing delinquency. Results in the former case are particularly discouraging, because this was an ambitious scheme to provide a long period of more or less continuous, highly personalized assistance based on a "directed friendship" model that hopefully would prove more effective than conventional social casework.[69] World War II interrupted the project, causing considerable disruption through staff turnover and entry of some of the treated boys into the armed forces. Whereas a ten-year treatment period had been planned, the median period of treatment actually received was about five years. Powers and Witmer found in the data comparing outcomes for the T-boys (experimental or treatment group) and the C-boys (the nontreated control group of otherwise similar "predelinquents") some favorable signs. Findings suggested that the later and more serious stages of delinquent careers may in some instances have been averted through the counseling efforts. Nor did they accept the argument that the "big brother" approach was sentimentalized or unprofessional (indeed they cite the fact that the most successful single counselor in the study was a nurse who had no professional social work training). On the whole, however, the impact of this ambitious counseling scheme was negligible:

> Throughout the treatment period the counselors were evidently
> not successful in preventing boys from committing offenses that
> brought them to the attention of the police in Cambridge (where

two-thirds of them resided). Indeed, the counselors seem to have had no positive effect whatever in this respect, as measured by the number of T-boys appearing before the Bureau in comparison with a matched group equal in number who did not receive this special counseling service. The number of boys who appeared, as well as the total number of appearances, was greater for the treatment group than for the control group. It can be said, nevertheless, that there was a *slight* preponderance of C-boys among the most active recidivists.[70]

Similarly disappointing results were noted in a New York project usually referred to as the Girls Vocational High Study.[71] In this research the high school in question identified girls with potential problems, and from among these it referred a random sample to a social work agency specializing in casework and group therapy with adolescent girls. Comparisons were made between the girls receiving such services and those in a control group that was drawn from the same pool but did not receive treatment. Apart from relatively less subsequent truancy among the treated girls—a finding that was stated cautiously, but which the researchers felt might have wide ramifications—a variety of objective measures failed to reveal significant differences between the groups of girls that might be attributable to the treatment.

> . . . On these tests no strong indications of effect are found and the conclusion must be stated in the negative when it is asked whether social work intervention with potential problem high school girls was in this instance effective.
>
> However, the evidence is not wholly negative. With due recognition of the very low magnitude of any relationship between experimental or control status of the cases and any of these criteria measures, it may be noted that the direction of many of them tends to favor girls who had the benefit of the treatment program. This may be little basis for enthusiasm . . . but it is not entirely discouraging. It testifies to the difficulty of changing deviant careers, a difficulty that is apparent whenever serious evaluative assessments have been undertaken.[72]

These major evaluation studies provide little general encouragement, then, for intensive counseling of potential delinquents. Without question, however, such services do produce favorable results in some individual cases. Furthermore, given the enormous interest recently in developing "community mental health" services that will actively seek out problem cases and undertake preventive measures, we can expect to see continued and intensified efforts to identify potential troublemakers and subject them to intensive treatment. Quite apart from their questionable assumptions, and their demonstrated ineffectiveness, there is a real danger of possible boomerang effects. Expressing grave concern about the role of psychiatry in the schools, and insisting that casting the child in a patient role is in fact stigmatizing, Szasz notes the impossibility of defense against psychiatric diagnoses that may cite almost any trait or behavior as an indicator of potential problems. "To categorize academic performance that is 'underachievement,' 'overachievement,' or 'erratic performance' as pathological would be humorous if it were not tragic. When we are told that if a psychiatric patient is early for his appointment he is anxious, if late he is hostile, and if on time, compulsive—we laugh, because it is supposed to be a joke. But here we are told the same thing in all seriousness." [73]

Even if one were to assume that the effects of early counseling or therapy were more often than not beneficial, there is reason for concern over the ways the existing programs are administered. According to one study of child-guidance clinics and court psychiatric clinics:

> There is good reason to believe that child-guidance agencies are not handling the very difficult cases or those in greatest need of help. First, a relatively small proportion of lower-class children apply to child-guidance agencies while the overwhelming majority of court-clinic cases come from lower-class families. Second, although delinquency reaches a peak at the age of fourteen, there is a gap in child-guidance services to those between eleven to fourteen years of age. Third, contrary to what might be expected, clients exhibiting behavior which violates the law will not necessarily, as a matter of course, be given priority in treatment.[74]

Actually, voluntary diversion to private agencies has long been one reason why middle-class children have had relatively low official delinquency rates. But critics will question whether the extension of psychiatric services to more lower-class children (who, as noted, are already especially susceptible to diagnosis by middle-class observers as troublemakers) is the best way of righting that disparity.

Similar to individual treatment is supervision on probation in lieu of commitment to a juvenile institution. As in voluntary referrals to counseling, the hope here, particularly with first offenders, is to "nip in the bud" the individual's delinquent proclivities. While officials and students of correction policies have long insisted that many inmates in institutions could be better helped in the community at large, there has been little clear evidence of the efficacy of particular probation techniques. In part, the assessment of probation methods is hampered by less than optimal working conditions. Probation programs are poorly supported and inadequately staffed, and as a result, the caseloads of probation officers are excessive.[75] Some of the difficulties imposed by the inadequate resources are nicely captured in two examples cited by the President's Crime Commission:

> A probation officer has arranged a meeting with a 16-year-old boy, on probation for car theft for the past 2 months. The boy begins to open up and talk for the first time. He explains that he began to "slip into the wrong crowd" a year or so after his stepfather died. He says that it would help to talk about it. But there isn't time; the waiting room is full, and the boy is not scheduled to come back for another 15-minute conference until next month.
>
> . . . A young, enthusiastic probation officer goes to see his supervisor and presents a plan for "something different," a group counseling session to operate three evenings a week for juvenile probationers and their parents. The supervisor tells him to forget it. "You've got more than you can handle now, getting up presentence reports for the judge. Besides, we don't have any extra budget for a psychiatrist to help out." [76]

Probation work is also plagued by vague goals and inappropriate techniques. Psychiatric social work—in which the assumptions and orientations of individual treatment are central—has provided a guiding model. According to one assessment made in 1960, the dominant view of probation reflected in the professional literature was as a form of treatment or casework, with a heavy stress on psychiatric perspectives. "The shift has been from a social to a clinical frame of reference. Crime and delinquency are acts containing social implications, but it is chiefly the individual personality which interests the caseworker." [77] The writer went on to note that this kind of casework was hampered by the same bad working conditions under which, in reality, probation can amount to "little more than administrative supervision." Furthermore, his study of a specific sample of juvenile court probationers disclosed that the greater the contact with probation officers, intensity of counseling, and referral to psychiatrists, the greater the subsequent records of criminality.[78]

Since then, it is possible that there has been a partial shift in probation programs away from a narrow emphasis on casework theories and practices. At the very least, quite different models of probation work have been proposed, as seen in this statement of the President's Crime Commission:

> . . . probation and parole would have wider functions than are now usually emphasized within their casework guidance orientation. They would have to take much more responsibility for such matters as seeing that offenders get jobs and settle into responsible work habits; arranging reentry into schools and remedial tutoring or vocational training; giving guidance and counseling to an offender's family; securing housing in a neighborhood without the temptations of bad companions; or getting a juvenile into neighborhood club activities or athletic teams.[79]

Although this conception of probation—in which the probation office is seen more as a general community assistance agency than as a therapy unit—veers away from the conventional idea of treatment, there is reason to believe that the casework approach continues to maintain a strong hold in the field. Probation work, therefore, is likely to have an uncertain and limited effectiveness because of its reliance on psychiatric formulations and treatment assumptions.

Recently great interest has been shown in community treatment programs. To an extent, some of these programs transcend the limitations of a narrow treatment emphasis, for they may be based on different assumptions about causation and take into account the individual's relation to the community and particularly to his peers. The features of individual treatment and those of liberal reform (to be considered in the next chapter) may tend to merge in this approach. Since, however, the basic focus in these programs remains on the treatment of individuals—even where treatment occurs in a community setting and involves recognizing community factors— it is appropriate to consider them in the present discussion.

One of the leading examples of community treatment is the program at Pinehills, in Provo, Utah.[80] Boys in this program spend only part of the day at the program center; they live in the community and are employed by the city and county in a variety of jobs in parks, streets, and recreation areas. Only twenty boys are assigned to this program at one time, and this group is broken down into two smaller discussion units. The daily group meetings of these units, adopting the techniques of "guided group interaction" (developed at Highfields), are the core of the program. Basically, the Provo program involves relatively unstructured, candid group sessions in which an effort is made to develop peer support for law-abiding values and to marshal group pressures as a deterrent to lapsing back into delinquency. The program has been limited to "habitual offenders," who are made aware that for them the alternative is the state training school. Length of stay in the program is unspecified, and the group itself has considerable authority to assess individual progress and determine readiness for release. The Provo scheme is interesting because, although in a way it is a kind of "group therapy," it is quite explicitly grounded in sociological assumptions (such as "delinquent value systems," the importance of the peer group, and the emphasis on work and adapting to the larger community). This also was one of the first such programs to have a research design; the adjudicated delinquents came from a general pool of eligibles that were randomly assigned to Provo, the state training school, or ordinary probation. While some criticize the Provo group sessions for using a kind of brainwashing, and while random assignment of youths to various programs according to research needs might also be considered objectionable, the experiment has provided good opportunity for comparative evaluation. According to a 1964 assessment, 84 percent of all boys completing the pro-

gram had gone without being rearrested during the six months following release. For the control group of regular probationers and
the control subjects in the state school the comparative figures were
77 percent and 42 percent, respectively.[81]

Also highly praised as an alternative to institutionalization has
been the Community Treatment Project of the California Youth Authority, which in its reliance on psychological formulations and personality assessment techniques much more directly reflects the individual treatment orientation.[82] Here again, youths from an eligible
pool (boys and girls undergoing first commitment from the juvenile
courts, but excluding certain serious offense categories) are randomly assigned to the experimental program and to the Authority's
regular probation program. The California scheme classifies its
subjects by means of the Interpersonal Maturity Level Classification.
Youths are categorized by "maturity levels," and nine related "delinquent subtypes" have been identified. A listing of these subtypes
immediately conveys the psychological emphasis of the program:[83]

Asocial, Aggressive
Asocial, Passive
Conformist, Immature
Conformist, Cultural
Manipulator
Neurotic, Acting-out
Neurotic, Anxious
Situational Emotional Reaction
Cultural Identifier

Most youths in the program live in their own homes, but some
are placed in foster or group homes. The treatment itself may be on
an individual or group basis (the treatment goals and methods vary
considerably among various subtypes within maturity levels), but
at least in the early stages the treatment is quite intensive. Community Agents, who usually concentrate on directing treatment for
only one or two of the subtypes, see each youth two to five times
weekly either individually or in group meetings. The average length

of stay in the program is about the same as for the Youth Authority's regular programs—around two years. A recent evaluation indicated that with respect to both parole success and personality test results (various tests are administered at intake and following treatment) the community program produced more favorable results than the regular one. As for parole success, the following data were reported:

> The failure rates (including all revocations of parole, recommitments from the courts, and unfavorable discharges) for *Control* cases are 52 percent (51 percent for boys, 57 percent for girls) after 15 months of community exposure time and 61 percent after 24 months of community exposure time. . . . In contrast, the failure rates for the *Experimental* cases are 28 percent (30 percent for boys, 13 percent for girls) at 15 months and 38 percent at 24 months. These Experimental-Control differences are highly significant statistically.[84]

Community treatment appeared to be more effective, however, in dealing with certain delinquent subtypes than with others. The highest success rate was for the "neurotic acting-out" category, the lowest for the "cultural identifiers" (this latter type "responds to identification with a deviant value system by living out his delinquent beliefs"). Such a difference seems quite predictable in the light of the program's heavy psychological-psychiatric emphasis. At least one critic, however, has challenged the overall evaluation of success in this project. Noting that the use of parole revocation as a criterion is questionable because violations might be differentially identified and reacted to under the two programs, Lerman (having reanalyzed data from the study) states: "the chance that an experimental boy's offense will be handled by revocation of parole is lower than for a control boy if the offense is low or moderate in seriousness; experimentals are judged similarly to the controls *only* when the offenses are of high seriousness. It is difficult not to conclude that the experimental boys have a lower parole-violation rate because offenses of low and medium seriousness are evaluated differently by adults according to organizational context." [85]

There are also "diversion" proposals designed to channel youthful offenders or potential offenders away from the criminal justice system and bring them under the jurisdiction of alternative programs. Lemert has provided a most useful summary and assessment of a great many of these schemes.[86] Programs in which youths in trouble increasingly would be dealt with in the schools, by state-run child welfare agencies, or by special bureaus within police departments may vary in the degree to which they employ personal counseling and stress psychological perspectives. All of them, however, do involve singling out, and doing something with or for, specific individuals; they are programs for dealing with delinquents, rather than with delinquency in some broader sense. Commenting on the Passaic Children's Bureau program, in which aggressive action by the local school system in dealing with truancy and other student problems led to apparent declines in (formally recorded) delinquency, Lemert states:

> The Passaic Bureau essentially achieves the goal of putting youth problems into a nonlegal context, and thus it may be said to divert cases otherwise destined for official court processing. Keeping truancy and student insubordination as clear responsibilities of the schools is an important means to this end. Arranging restitution through Bureau auspices is another way of encouraging normal community problem-solving in cases of property destruction. How far the work of the Bureau reduces the volume of youth problems through direct normalization, writing off, as it were, minor deviance, or raising community tolerance for it, cannot be determined. Stressing early detection and prevention, which apparently is part of Bureau policy, works at opposing purposes.[87]

Probation-type work by police children's bureaus or police "liason" schemes (such as the one originated in Liverpool, England), and the creation of special child welfare councils (as in the Scandinavian countries) to take over much of the present jurisdiction of juvenile courts,[88] similarly may provide alternatives to formal legal procedures and training schools. Against the possibility of effective and nonstigmatizing early assistance, however, must be set the likelihood of distinct intervention in the lives of children without the benefit of legal safeguards. Indeed, the nonlegalistic options may increase the incidence of intervention, given the ideas about early identification and prevention that they incorporate. It should however be recognized that there may be some relative advantage (in terms of juveniles' attitudes and self-concepts) to intervention by agencies and agents of social control that are not associated in the youth's mind with the apparatus of law enforcement and the courts. Thus, one study found that adjudicated delinquents had relatively favorable attitudes toward probation officers (and even more favorable ones toward mental health professionals) because they did not seem part of the regular criminal justice apparatus; likewise, they reacted more favorably to special juvenile officers than to ordinary police officers.[89]

To what extent the Youth Services Bureau, a diversion mechanism strongly endorsed by the President's Crime Commission, would adopt individual treatment practices is not clear. As described by the Commission, such a bureau might emphasize counseling, or it might deal with delinquency problems through community action and organization. A primary function, the commission suggested, would be "individually tailored work with troublemaking youths," but it went on to note that such work "might include group and individual counseling, placement in group and foster homes, work and recreational programs, employment counseling, and special education (remedial, vocational). . . . The key to the bureau's success would be voluntary participation by the juvenile and his family in working out and following a plan of service or rehabilitation." [90] Lemert comments that it is really too early to assess youth service bureaus, as they are just beginning to be organized, but he is little encouraged by the preliminary steps he has observed in California. Noting that general discussions of these bureaus have pointed out the serious issues of "their sources of authority, means of support, professional tone, and their relationships to existing agencies," he sees a substantial risk that they "will become just one more community agency following popular or fashionable trends in youth work, muddying the waters a little more and falling into obscurity." With respect to the California efforts he states: "It is hard to escape the impression of old ideas being recycled when looking at the organizational plan of some of the Bureaus." [91]

INSTITUTIONAL TREATMENT

It is not possible, in this relatively brief essay, to review comprehensively the voluminous professional literature on correctional institutions.[92] However certain aspects of juvenile institutions and their programs are particularly germane to our discussion of the treatment model. The notion of segregating troublesome youth from the rest of the citizenry in hopes of reforming them through "rehabilitative" regimes is of course a basic feature of this model. Special juvenile institutions were supposed to provide a protective environment where problem children would be shielded both from bad home and neighborhood influences, and from the adult offenders incarcerated in regular jails and prisons. Unfortunately, as is now widely recognized, this scheme confronted from the outset (and it continues to confront) some extremely serious obstacles.

Some of these perennial problems are quite mundane. Juvenile facilities are inadequate, unevenly distributed, and poorly supported.[93] From the standpoint of administering juvenile justice, these basic problems are more serious than they appear. Not only are children put through badly deficient programs, but often the dispositions in juvenile justice (assignment to and release from programs) are governed by practical exigencies. Thus, commitment of a specific youth to a particular training school may have less to do with the type of program available there, or how it answers his situation and problems, than with the issue of where there is room for him in that particular jurisdiction. Whether to commit him to a training school at all or instead put him on probation may hinge on the availability and distribution of scarce resources. The resource factor is not just a matter of the quality and distribution of services; because of its influence on disposition patterns, it also affects official delinquency statistics and makes questionable the causation theories derived from them.

Organizational research and theorizing have thrown new light on such treatment-related features of juvenile institutions as: development and influence of inmate social structure, multiplicity of institutional goals, problems of interaction within the institution (between different types of staff, as well as between staff and inmates), and the institution's relationships with external forces.

The early aim of treating juveniles in special institutions that somehow would not become "schools for crime" is now widely seen as unrealistic. Even in loosely structured institutions, difficulties are created by the inevitable development among the inmates of informal social organization and informal systems of norms and sanctions. The inmates and staff contrast sharply in their basic values and social backgrounds. Furthermore, as Polsky found in his observational research on cottage social systems, "The drastic restrictions for achieving status within the cottage lead to exaggerated conformity with peer-group standards. These rigid patterns sharply limit the possibilities of personality experimentation and social change. A powerful reference group is thus created and interposed between the child and the staff, and challenges that staff's practices, values, and aspirations." [94] Possibly the pressures for accommodation between these divergent systems are somewhat less severe in some juvenile institutions than in adult (and particularly maximum security) prisons, where what has been termed "the corruption of authority" (the willingness of guards to ignore considerable violations in exchange for cooperation) is common. But, as one close student of juvenile institutions has asserted, "Some kind of *modus vivendi* must be reached between client leadership and staff in any institution if perpetual crisis is to be avoided." [95] These problems have shaped professional and official views on the organization and administration of juvenile institutions. Such trends as considering the entire institutional "milieu" to be part of the treatment, developing nonauthoritarian "collaborative" modes of organization, and marshaling peer-group opinion in the interest of treatment goals (as in the "guided group interaction" schemes)—all seek to undermine or alter the potentially subversive impact of the inmate culture.

Also plaguing juvenile institutions have been difficulties stemming from the apparently contradictory goals of treatment and custody. Whereas most institutions now give at least lip service to the goals of treatment and rehabilitation, in fact guiding perspectives and actual practices vary considerably. Several factors (such as inadequate resources, community pressures, and the orientations of specific administrators) limit the extent to which purely custodial efforts can be discarded. According to one major survey:

> . . . we estimate that at least half of public institutions are basically custodial (obedience/conformity format) and have only limited features of the reeducation/development format. At least another 25 percent of the institutions have moved to the reeducation/development level, whereas the remainder have substantial features of the treatment organization.[96]

These conflicts are seen most clearly in the confused and strained relations between custodial staff (primarily "cottage parents") and professional treatment personnel. Often the cottage parents feel they have built up a wealth of "know-how" in their daily contacts with the juveniles, and they resent many of the innovative efforts by the "ivory tower" staff of professionals. Whereas the treatment staff feel the nonprofessionals believe in simplistic and disciplinary solutions to problems of the children in their care, the cottage parents insist they are closer to the real situation: "It's fine and easy for you people working up in the administration building to come at eight o'clock, leave at five, and have a half-day off on Saturday, but we cottage parents are with the boys all the time. If we aren't, one of our helpers is." [97] It is ironic, that the staff members, who have the most continuous contact with the inmates, are the least likely to accept the most up-to-date treatment philosophies and techniques. Furthermore, this continuous contact implies a special danger, that a sort of cooptation by the inmates may occur:

> The cottage parent's personality predispositions, his isolation from the professional staff, and the intense interaction with twenty disturbed delinquents [in the institution Polsky studied] results in a role adaptation which alienates him from the relevant professional structures and philosophy of the treatment institution. Lacking an alternative status reference group, the cottage parent becomes dependent upon, and conforming to, the boys' delinquent orientation and eventually adjusts to it by taking over and utilizing modified delinquent techniques. The extreme concern with cottage loyalty and the violent condemnation of

"ratting" cement the cottage parent to the boys' subculture and
perpetuate a vicious circle which insulates the cottage from the
rest of the therapeutic milieu.[98]

Presumably, this is one variety of *modus vivendi* Zald had in mind
in making the statement about staff-client accommodation cited
earlier. Efforts to develop new kinds of informal, nonauthoritarian
"team" treatment organization may reduce some of these strains and
conflicts. The very process of innovation may, however, impose
strains of its own. Thus, a study of one institution found that when
a new and more treatment-oriented administration and program
were suddenly introduced, with attempts to integrate professional
and nonprofessional roles, cottage parents found themselves expected to perform in unfamiliar and unwanted ways. As a result,
they displayed not only signs of irritation and rebellion, but also
patterns of withdrawal and even psychosomatic symptoms.[99] Notwithstanding various reforms and efforts at education, very likely it
is still true that in large, traditional institutions conflicts between
professionals and nonprofessionals can render "constructive interaction among staff . . . nearly impossible." [100]

Even if an institution were able to surmount the multiple-goal
problem in order to concentrate on treatment, and if it also could
deal smoothly with the complex interrelationships it must maintain
with outside forces (legislatures, other community agencies and institutions, "public opinion") there still would remain great uncertainty regarding the ingredients of a successful treatment program.
Numerous types of institutions and treatment schemes exist, each
with its proponents and each with its claims to varying degrees of
success.[101] Furthermore, to the extent one accepts treatment goals
at all, there may well be need for a variety of treatment types and
subtypes, such as for the variations in offense patterns mentioned
earlier. However, almost all the claims to success must be viewed
with great caution. Most of the "evaluation studies" are subject to a
variety of methodological criticisms,[102] and not the least of the
reasons for caution is the fact that many of these studies have been
undertaken by personnel of the programs being evaluated—who
understandably have a professional and even personal stake in the
outcomes.

Consequently, statements about the relative merits of different approaches—small units versus big units, well-structured versus loosely organized programs, group-work versus individual therapy, and so on—cannot really be made with any certainty. Nonetheless, some trends are clearly discernible. With respect to residential institutions, there is a growing preference for relatively small units, organized on nonauthoritarian "collaborative" principles, in which the treatment rests on the design and impact of the entire milieu, and often uses the guided group interaction technique. The major model for this approach has been the early Highfields experiment in New Jersey.[103] Highfields has attempted a short-term (three to four months) treatment program with a limited number of boys (twenty at a time). Housed on a former estate, the boys work during the day at a nearby mental hospital and attend group meetings in the evening. The regime is quite informal and flexible, with few of the trappings of the ordinary correctional institution. Guided group interaction as developed there, and so named in order to indicate that the process involved is something other than traditional group therapy, emphasizes the group process itself and not simply the treatment of the individual members. It is intended to provide a relatively informal, supportive, democratic atmosphere for group exploration.

> It assumes the delinquent will benefit from a social experience where, in concert with his peers and the leader, he can freely discuss, examine, and understand his problems of living, without the threats that had been so common in his previous learning experiences. It further assumes that the mutual "give and take" of group discussion stimulates the delinquent to some understanding of the relationship between what takes place in this learning situation and his immediate problems of living. Therefore, the relationships encountered and the material discussed must be felt by the participant as making some contribution to his critical struggle for adjustment.[104]

Because there was not random assignment of cases to Highfields and to Annandale, the state training school with which comparisons were made, the claim of differential effectiveness must be tempered by awareness of differences between the two innate populations.

Boys sent to Highfields were younger than those sent to Annandale, were likely to have had completed more schooling, and were all first offenders. Subject however to a number of methodological limitations, some of which they themselves acknowledged, the Highfields researchers claimed considerable success for the program. Thus, of all boys sent to the project during the study period, 63 in every 100 Highfields boys, and only 47 of every 100 Annandale boys, completed treatment and did not require reinstitutionalization. When the analysis eliminated cases of boys returned to the court, and focused only on the boys who completed treatment, the apparent success rate was even higher: "for every hundred boys who complete residence in the respective facility, the Highfields program rehabilitates twenty-eight more than does the traditional program of caring for such boys." [105]

While the trend in juvenile institutions clearly seems to be away from individual therapy and toward group discussions in what is hoped to be a more encompassing "therapeutic milieu," the latter approach is sometimes difficult to adopt. As one might expect, this is particularly true where a new regime is being substituted for a more traditional one in an existing institution. The problems involved often go beyond the treatment-custodial conflicts mentioned above. Thus Street, Winter, and Perrow note:

> . . . difficulty in developing elaborated notions of milieu treatment when the clinical personnel were dominantly schooled in and attuned to orientations appropriate to two-person therapy. Milton [one of the institutions studied] had explicitly given up individual counseling as the major mode of treatment and attempted to work mainly through cottage committee meetings with inmate and group therapy sessions. Yet many of the clinical staff members seemed insensitive to group phenomena. . . . Several staff members expressed enthusiasm over our telling them about "inmate informal organization," a concept they said they were eager to consider. Many of the professional personnel thought of most of the inmates as emotionally disturbed. [106]

Even though rehabilitation programs (including those in residential settings) are trying to move away from at least some aspects of individual treatment, this orientation dies hard. Increasingly, corrections officials are looking with favor on reforms moving one step further, toward nonresidential programs like the Pinehills and California community treatment model. Many have now recognized that "regardless of the type of program investigated, residential institutions for delinquents (under eighteen years of age) are characterized by high rates of potential failure." [107] It remains to be seen whether anything more optimistic can be said about the community treatment efforts. It also remains to be seen whether such efforts— which as noted above could move in any number of different directions—will succeed in casting off some of their unrealistic assumptions and techniques.

INDIVIDUALIZED JUSTICE

As should now be quite apparent, there is a strong link between the individual treatment reaction and the philosophy and practice of the traditional juvenile court. Work of this specialized tribunal, which under the concept of *parens patriae* would intervene for the state as a parent, rested heavily on the "rehabilitative ideal." [108] To the reformers who founded the original juvenile courts, it was an article of faith (almost literally, one might add) that the causes of youth problems and wrongdoing could be scientifically identified and treated. Furthermore, the therapeutic measures employed "should be designed to effect changes in the behavior of the convicted person in the interests of his own happiness, health, and satisfactions and in the interest of social defense." [109]

Delinquency, then, was seen as a symptom of some treatable disorder, and the judicial mechanisms themselves were geared to rooting out the underlying causes. This was the basis for the "personalized" or "individualized' justice that was supposed to be the distinctive quality of the juvenile court.[110] The problems and situation of each child brought before the court were to be considered in depth, and efforts made to adopt a program of rehabilitation suited to the particular child's needs. These needs, rather than the details of whatever specific incident gave rise to the court hearing in the first place, constituted the major concern of the court, for the focus was on antecedent root causes. The very wording of the juvenile statutes—which enable the court to intervene at the slightest sign of trouble or misbehavior—indicates the hope that these tribunals would undertake this kind of far-reaching assessment in individual cases. It may be significant, in this connection, that the first juvenile court act (in Illinois, in 1899) even authorized penalties for "predelinquent" behavior.[111]

In line with this perspective, in which the child was seen as being not responsible for his act, and indeed the act itself was only a secondary concern, there was to be no finding of "guilt" such as occurred in the criminal courts. Rather, a child would be "adjudicated" a delinquent, in need of help, and a program of rehabilitation prescribed in his interests. Since the procedural rigidity of the ordinary criminal trial would interfere with this free-wheeling evaluation of the child's needs, that too would be discarded in favor of an exploratory and nonadversary process. Finally, and again following the implications of the rehabilitative ideal, commitment to treatment would be indeterminate, since the treatment specialists would be in the best position to know just when the particular child's needs had been met.

Later on, we shall consider briefly some of the numerous criticisms of these procedures. But in terms of our broader focus on major patterns of reaction to delinquency, the apparent reciprocal influence between the individual treatment response and the traditional juvenile court system may be of even greater interest. Treatment outlooks (involving the assumptions of individual determinism and the focus on differentiation between supposed offenders and nonoffenders) helped shape our juvenile justice system, and continue to support it. At the same time, the processing mechanisms themselves, accorded legitimacy as an accepted albeit much criticized part of the legal system, may have reinforced the treatment orientation. This intermeshing of generalized outlooks and specific legal institutions has to be taken into account in any efforts to develop new ways of dealing with "delinquency" problems.

✠ ✠ ✠

1. David Matza, *Delinquency and Drift* (New York: John Wiley & Sons, Inc., 1964), pp. 11–12.

2. *Ibid.*, pp. 6, 8.

3. Don C. Gibbons. *Delinquent Behavior* (Englewood Cliffs, N.J.: Prentice-Hall, Inc., 1970), p. 75.

4. For discussion of the biological theories, see George B. Vold, *Theoretical Criminology* (New York: Oxford University Press, 1958); also Edwin M. Schur, *Our Criminal Society* (Englewood Cliffs, N.J.: Prentice-Hall, Inc., 1969), pp. 55–61; and Martin, Fitzpatrick, *Delinquent Behavior* (New York: Random House, Inc., 1964), pp. 124–31.

5. Jane E. Brody, "Experts Now Link a Learning Disorder to Delinquency," *The New York Times*, February 13, 1972, p. 46.

6. *Ibid.*

7. Sheldon and Eleanor Glueck, *Physique and Delinquency* (New York: Harper & Row, Publishers, 1956).

8. *Delinquent Behavior*, p. 76.

9. Travis Hirschi and Hanan C. Selvin, *Delinquency Research: An Appraisal of Analytic Methods* (New York: Free Press, 1967), pp. 96–97.

10. William and Joan McCord, *The Psychopath* (Princeton, N.J.: D. Van Nostrand, Co., Inc., 1964), p. 3; originally published as *Psychopathy and Delinquency* (New York: Grune and Stratton, Inc., 1956). For further discussion of psychopathy, see Hervey Cleckly, *The Mask of Sanity* (St. Louis: The C. V. Mosby Co., 1941); and Robert M. Lindner, *Rebel Without a Cause* (New York: Grune and Stratton, Inc., 1944).

11. McCord, *Psychopath*, p. 85.

12. Alfred R. Lindesmith, "The Drug Addict as Psychopath," *American Sociological Review*, 5 (1940), 920.

13. McCord, *Psychopath*, pp. 40, 41.

14. See, for example, Harrison C. Gough, "A Sociological Theory of Psychopathy," *American Journal of Sociology*, 53 (March, 1948), 359–66.

15. Lee N. Robins, *Deviant Children Grown Up* (Baltimore: The Williams & Wilkins Co., 1966).

16. Gibbons, *Delinquent Behavior*, p. 86.

17. McCord, *Psychopath*, pp. 51, 52.

18. Franz Alexander and Hugo Staub, *The Criminal, the Judge and the Public*, rev. ed., tr. G. Zilboorg (New York: Collier Books, 1962), pp. 51–52.

19. Matza, *Delinquency and Drift*, p. 17.

20. For examples of early psychological approaches to delinquency, see August Aichhorn, *Wayward Youth* (New York: The Viking Press, 1935); Kate Friedlander, *The Psychoanalytic Approach to Juvenile Delinquency* (New York: International Universities Press, 1947); William

Healy and Augusta F. Bronner, *New Light on Delinquency and Its Treatment* (New Haven: Yale University Press, 1936).

21. See, for example, Fritz Redl and David Wineman, *Children Who Hate* (New York: Collier Books, 1962).

22. This increased openness and flexibility toward sociological factors in causation is illustrated by the work of Richard L. Jenkins. See his *Breaking Patterns of Defeat* (Philadelphia: J. B. Lippincott Co., 1954); also discussion of his work, and the numerous journal articles cited therein, in Gibbons, *Delinquent Behavior*, pp. 88–89.

23. General sociological assessments, and reference to additional specific studies can be found in Vold, *Theoretical Criminology*, Ch. 7; Gibbons, *Delinquent Behavior*, pp. 76–89; Martin, Fitzpatrick, *Delinquent Behavior*, pp. 131–138; and Schur, *Our Criminal Society*, pp. 61–73; see also Barbara Wooton, *Social Science and Social Pathology* (London: Macmillan & Co., Ltd., 1959).

24. Albert K. Cohen, "The Sociology of the Deviant Act: Anomie Theory and Beyond," *American Sociological Review*, 30 (February, 1965), 9.

25. Howard S. Becker, *Outsiders* (New York: Free Press, 1963), p. 23.

26. Albert K. Cohen, *Deviance and Control* (Englewood Cliffs, N.J.: Prentice-Hall, Inc., 1966), p. 44.

27. See Karl F. Schuessler and Donald R. Cressey, "Personality Characteristics of Criminals," *American Journal of Sociology*, 55 (March, 1950), 476–84; also Gordon P. Waldo and Simon Dinitz, "Personality Attributes of the Criminal: An Analysis of Research Studies, 1950–1965," *Journal of Research in Crime and Delinquency*, 4 (July, 1967), 185–202.

28. Thomas S. Szasz, *The Myth of Mental Illness* (New York: Hoeber, 1961); and *Ideology and Insanity*, Anchor Books (New York: Doubleday & Company, Inc., 1970).

29. Szasz, *Ideology and Insanity*, p. 3.

30. See Walter Reckless, Simon Dinitz, and Ellen Murray, "Self-Concept as an Insulator Against Delinquency," *American Sociological Review*, 21 (December, 1956), 744–46; Reckless, Dinitz, and Barbara Kay, "The Self Component in Potential Delinquency and Potential Non-Delinquency," *American Sociological Review*, 22 (October, 1957), 566–70; and other reports by Reckless, Dinitz, Scarpatti, et al., cited below.

31. Isidor Chein, et al., *The Road to H: Narcotics, Delinquency, and Social Policy* (New York: Basic Books, Inc., 1964).

32. Talcott Parsons, "Certain Primary Sources and Patterns of Aggression in the Social Structure of the Western World," *Psychiatry*, 10 (May, 1947), 167–81.

33. Albert K. Cohen, *Delinquent Boys: The Culture of the Gang* (New York: Free Press, 1955), p. 164.

34. See Reckless, et al., "Self Concept as an Insulator," Albert J. Reiss, Jr., "Delinquency as the Failure of Personal and Social Controls," *American Sociological Review*, 16 (1951), 196–207; F. Ivan Nye, *Family Relationships and Delinquent Behavior* (New York: John Wiley & Sons, Inc., 1958); and Hirschi, *Causes of Delinquency.*

35. Sheldon and Eleanor Glueck, *Unraveling Juvenile Delinquency* (New York: Commonwealth Fund, 1950).

36. See, for example, John Bowlby, *Child Care and the Growth of Love* (London: Penguin Books, 1953).

37. See Glueck, *Unraveling Juvenile Delinquency*; Nye, *Family Relationships*; Martin Gold, *Status Forces in Delinquent Boys* (Ann Arbor, Mich.: Institute of Social Research, 1963); Nye and Lois W. Hoffman, eds., *The Employed Mother in America* (Skokie, Ill.: Rand McNally & Co., 1963).

38. Hyman Rodman and Paul Grams, "Juvenile Delinquency and the Family: A Review and Discussion," in President's Commission on Law Enforcement and Administration of Justice, *Task Force Report: Juvenile Delinquency and Youth Crime* (Washington, D.C.: U.S. Government Printing Office, 1967), pp. 196–97.

39. Hirschi and Selvin, *Delinquency Research*, p. 97.

40. Rodman and Grams, "Juvenile Delinquency and the Family."

41. *Ibid.*

42. *Ibid.*, p. 215.

43. Jackson Toby, "An Evaluation of Early Identification and Intensive Treatment Programs for Predelinquents," in John R. Stratton and Robert M. Terry, eds., *Prevention of Delinquency* (New York: The Macmillan Company, 1968), pp. 99–116.

44. Starke R. Hathaway and Elio D. Monachesi, "The Personalities of Predelinquent Boys," in Stratton and Terry, eds., *Prevention of Delinquency*, p. 64.

45. Toby, "Early Identification," p. 101.

46. Edwin Powers and Helen Witmer, *An Experiment in the Prevention of Delinquency* (New York: Columbia University Press, 1951); for a further analysis of data from the study, see William and Joan McCord, with Irving K. Zola, *Origins of Crime* (New York: Columbia University Press, 1959).

47. See Maude M. Craig and Selma J. Glick, "Ten Years Experience with the Glueck Social Prediction Scale," *Crime and Delinquency*, 9 (July, 1963), 249–61.

48. Robert E. Stanfield and Brendan Maher, "Clinical and Actuarial Prediction of Juvenile Delinquency," in Stanton Wheeler, ed., *Controlling Delinquents* (New York: John Wiley & Sons, Inc., 1968), p. 257.

49. Don M. Gottfredson, "Assessment and Prediction Methods in Crime and Delinquency," in President's Commission on Law Enforcement and Administration of Justice, *Task Force Report: Juvenile Delinquency and Youth Crime*, pp. 171–87.

50. Michael Hakeem, "A Critique of the Psychiatric Approach to the Prevention of Juvenile Delinquency," *Social Problems*, 5 (Winter, 1957–58), 194–205.

51. Stanfield and Maher, "Clinical and Actuarial Prediction," p. 251.

52. Craig and Glick, "Ten Years Experience."

53. See discussion in Toby, "Early Identification," and Gottfredson, "Assessment and Prediction Methods"; also Alfred J. Kahn, "The Case of the Premature Claims," *Crime and Delinquency*, 11 (July, 1965), 217–28.

54. Toby, "Early Identification," p. 108.

55. Hirschi and Selvin, *Delinquency Research.*

56. Toby, "Early Identification," p. 116.

57. An excellent discussion of the numerous methodological issues surrounding prediction is provided by Gottfredson, "Assessment and Prediction Methods"; see also Hermann Mannheim and Leslie T. Wilkins, *Prediction Methods in Relation to Borstal Training* (London: Her Majesty's Stationery Office, 1955).

58. Quoted in Kahn, "Premature Claims."

59. Charles Witter, "Drugging and Schooling," *Trans-action*, 8 (July–August, 1971), 31.

60. See cases cited by Nat Hentoff, "Drug-Pushing in the Schools: The Professionals," *The Village Voice*, May 25 and June 1, 1972.

61. John Holt, quoted in Witter, "Drugging and Schooling," p. 32.

62. Hentoff, "Drug-Pushing," *Village Voice*, May 25, 1972, pp. 20–21.

63. Ralph K. Schwitzgebel, *Development and Legal Regulation of Coercive Behavior Modification Techniques with Offenders*, Center for Studies of Crime and Delinquency, National Institute of Mental Health (Washington: U.S. Government Printing Office, 1971), p. 5.

64. *Ibid.*, pp. 7–8.

65. *Ibid.*, p. 8.

66. *Ibid.*, p. 17.

67. *Ibid.*, p. 20.

68. *Ibid.*, pp. 65, 66.

69. Powers and Witmer, *Prevention of Delinquency.*

70. *Ibid.*, p. 325.

71. Henry J. Meyer, Edgar F. Borgatta, and Wyatt C. Jones, *Girls at Vocational High: An Experiment in Social Work Intervention* (New York: Russell Sage Foundation, 1965).

72. *Ibid.*, p. 180.

73. Szasz, *Ideology and Insanity*, p. 150.

74. James E. Teele and Sol Levine, "The Acceptance of Emotionally Disturbed Children by Psychiatric Agencies," in Wheeler, *Controlling Delinquents*, pp. 123–24.

75. For statistics on probation resources and assessment of their significance, see President's Commission on Law Enforcement and Administration of Justice, *Task Force Report: Corrections* (Washington, D.C.: U.S. Government Printing Office, 1967), pp. 27–37; and pp. 130–41 (data from National Council on Crime and Delinquency survey, "Correction in the United States").

76. *Ibid.*, p. 5.

77. Lewis Diana, "What is Probation?," *Journal of Criminal Law, Criminology, and Police Science*, 51 (July–August, 1960), 189–204; reprinted in Giallombardo, ed., *Juvenile Delinquency*, p. 404.

78. *Ibid.*, pp. 411–12.

79. President's Commission on Law Enforcement and Administration of Justice, *Task Force Report: Corrections*, p. 9.

80. LaMar T. Empey and Jerome Rabow, "The Provo Experiment in Delinquency Rehabilitation," *American Sociological Review*, 26 (October, 1961), 679–95.

81. President's Commission, *Task Force Report: Corrections*, p. 39. A similar program has been developed at Essexfields, New Jersey. For general discussion of these and related types of programs (including relatively informal "residential group centers"), see LaMar T. Empey, "Alternatives to Incarceration," in Lerman, ed., *Delinquency and Social Policy*, pp. 298–317.

82. Marguerite Q. Warren, "The Community Treatment Project," in Norman Johnston, Leonard Savitz, and Marvin Wolfgang, eds., *The Sociology of Punishment and Correction*, 2nd ed. (New York: John Wiley & Sons, Inc., 1970), pp. 671–83.

83. *Ibid.*, p. 675.

84. *Ibid.*, p. 676.

85. Paul Lerman, "Evaluative Studies of Institutions for Delinquents," in Lerman, ed., *Delinquency and Social Policy*, p. 319.

86. Edwin M. Lemert, *Instead of Court: Diversion in Juvenile Jus-

tice, Center for Studies of Crime and Delinquency, National Institute of Mental Health (Washington, D.C.: U.S. Government Printing Office, 1971).

87. *Ibid.*, p. 33.

88. See discussion in *ibid.*, Chs. 3 and 4.

89. Brendan Maher, with Ellen Stein, "The Delinquent's Perception of the Law and the Community," in Wheeler, *Controlling Delinquents*, pp. 187–221.

90. President's Commission, *Task Force Report: Juvenile Delinquency and Youth Crime*, p. 20.

91. Lemert, *Instead of Court*, p. 93.

92. For major sociological perspectives see Johnston, Savitz, and Wolfgang, eds., *The Sociology of Punishment and Correction*; Gibbons, *Changing the Lawbreaker*; and Donald R. Cressey, ed., *The Prison: Studies in Institutional Organization and Change* (New York: Holt, Rinehart and Winston, Inc., 1961). An important comparative survey is reported on by David Street, Robert D. Winter, and Charles Perrow, *Organization for Treatment: A Comparative Study of Institutions for Delinquents* (New York: Free Press, 1966).

93. President's Commission, *Task Force Report: Corrections*, pp. 141–49.

94. Howard W. Polsky, *Cottage Six: The Social System of Delinquent Boys in Residential Treatment*, Wiley Science Editions (New York: John Wiley & Sons, Inc, 1965), p. 88.

95. Mayer Zald, "The Correctional Institution for Juvenile Offenders: An Analysis of Organizational 'Character'," in Lawrence Hazelrigg, ed., *Prison Within Society*, Anchor Books (New York: Doubleday & Company, Inc., 1969), p. 243.

96. Morris Janowitz, Foreword to Street, Winter, and Perrow, *Organization for Treatment*, p. xi.

97. Quoted by George H. Weber, "Conflicts Between Professional and Nonprofessional Personnel in Institutional Delinquency Treatment," in Hazelrigg, ed., *Prison Within Society*, p. 429.

98. Polsky, *Cottage Six*, p. 135.

99. George E. Weber, "Emotional and Defensive Reactions of Cottage Parents," in Cressey, ed., *The Prison*, pp. 189–228.

100. Weber, "Conflicts Between Professional and Nonprofessional Personnel," in Hazelrigg, ed., *Prison Within Society*, p. 442.

101. For a review of the major types of treatment see Gibbons, *Changing the Lawbreaker* (Englewood Cliffs, N.J.: Prentice-Hall, 1965), Ch. 4.

102. Lerman, "Evaluative Studies of Institutions for Delinquents," in *Delinquency and Social Policy*, pp. 317–28.

103. Lloyd W. McCorkle, Albert Elias, and F. Lovell Bixby, *The Highfields Story: An Experimental Treatment Project for Youthful Offenders* (New York: Henry Holt, 1958); and H. Ashley Weeks, *Youthful Offenders at Highfields: An Evaluation of the Effects of the Short-term Treatment of Delinquent Boys*, Ann Arbor Paperbacks (Ann Arbor: University of Michigan Press, 1968).

104. McCorkle, Elias, and Bixby, *Highlands Story*, p. 74.

105. Weeks, *Youthful Offenders*, pp. 119, 120.

106. Street, Winter, and Perrow, *Organization for Treatment*, p. 185.

107. Lerman, "Evaluative Studies of Institutions for Delinquents," in *Delinquency and Social Policy*, p. 317.

108. Francis A. Allen, *The Borderland of Criminal Justice* (Chicago: University of Chicago Press, 1964), pp. 25–41.

109. *Ibid.*, p. 26.

110. Gustav L. Schramm, "Philosophy of the Juvenile Court," *Annals of the American Academy of Political and Social Science*, 261 (January, 1949), 101–8.

111. Platt, *The Child Savers: The Invention of Delinquency* (Chicago: University of Chicago Press, 1969), p. 138.

REFORMING SOCIETY

The reform outlook is grounded in sociological studies of urban life and social class structure. Social determinism is a central organizing idea in this response pattern. Studies that underlie and support the reform reaction still rest on a belief that delinquents can be distinguished from nondelinquents, but now in terms of the social conditions to which they have been exposed, rather than individual characteristics. Thus, while questions of causation are not dismissed, ways of framing and exploring the questions and the kinds of answers that result are quite different.

If in both research and public policy the key reference point for the treatment reaction is the "delinquent" himself, the reform response devotes greater attention to the social class system, the neighborhood setting, and the group and subcultural contexts of youthful behavior. David Matza notes that sociological approaches to delinquency in general (not all of which, however, fit equally well for our purposes with the reform model), tend to be grounded in epidemiology,

> . . . the study of contrasting rates of pathology in different so-
> cial areas. Social theory begins with the observation that there
> are gross differences in the rate of delinquency by class, by
> ethnic affiliation, by rural or urban residence, by region, and
> perhaps by nation and historical epoch. From these gross differ-
> ences, the sociologist infers that something beyond the intimacy
> of family surroundings is operative in the emergence of delin-
> quent patterns; something in the cultural and social atmosphere
> apparent in certain sectors of society.[1]

Because of the concern with rate variations, tremendous emphasis has been placed in these analyses on the socioeconomic distribution of delinquency. The sociological theories from which reform
implications most directly stem either assert or assume that delinquency is heavily concentrated at the lower end of the socioeconomic spectrum. This assumption is not, of course, a prerequisite for
favoring liberal reform policies, but the belief that delinquency is
primarily a working-class or lower-class phenomenon does reinforce such preferences. As we shall see in Chapter Five, there is an
alternative view, based on considerable research data, that in fact
the behaviors we now call delinquency are extremely common
throughout the entire society, and are not necessarily concentrated
in the working-class sector. Proponents of this argument criticize unquestioning acceptance of the official statistics on delinquency because of their methodological inadequacy. On the other hand, few
of these critics would deny that there is indeed a great deal of working-class delinquency, however much there also may be in other
segments of the population. Similarly, for the most part they would
not oppose most liberal proposals for general socioeconomic reform, although they would not see it as the solution to delinquency
problems, and they might well oppose some of the specific delinquency programs that reformists advocate.

Since the focus is on the sociocultural context of delinquency
rather than the individual offender, these policies aim at changing
groups and neighborhoods as well as the social structure and value
systems of the society as a whole. Efforts of this sort (including

street-gang work, programs to widen educational and employment opportunities, and community organization schemes) receive support from the reformists' optimism about eradicating delinquency. If the basic causes of delinquent behavior are found in objective social and economic conditions, rather than within the personalties of particular individuals, then public policies to reduce delinquency should be relatively accessible. Yet even ardent reformers now realize that while ameliorating the underlying conditions may be a realistic goal, eliminating delinquency is not. Furthermore, proponents of individual treatment continually confront reformers with the argument that their measures, though perhaps quite commendable, evade the issue of individual differences in behavior and ignore questions of personal responsibility.

There are limits, then, on how far beyond the individual treatment approach the reform model can take us. Certainly the perspectives on delinquency have expanded to the extent that the individual offender is viewed in some relation to his social position and surroundings. Sociological formulations have also been helpful in undermining assumptions of individual pathology, and hence in reducing reliance on an unwieldy "medical model." Yet if some of these formulations have helped us overcome the "evil causes evil" fallacy, others have uncritically substituted notions of social pathology for those of individual disturbance. The idea remains that delinquency must be due to some disorder, some kind of malfunctioning. Furthermore, under this approach, we still encounter deterministic conceptions of the delinquent. Although the forces pushing a person into delinquency are now seen to be sociocultural rather than individual, "external" rather than "internal," the belief in a considerable amount of personal constraint remains. Indeed, the reform outlook to a large extent rests on the notion of structured variations in the freedom of individuals to shape their own destinies.

Above all, the reformist continues to see delinquency as a problem about which something must be done. It remained for those I call the "radical noninterventionists" to question this basic contention. As we shall see in Chapter Five, their argument for accommodating the system to a greater diversity of youthful behavior rests not only on the unworkability of and possible harms produced by present policies, but also upon research that challenges many of the basic reformist assumptions (including the distribution of delinquency and the constraint of the individual). Before turning to the developments that have nurtured this alternative outlook, however, we should examine the theoretical groundings of typical reform policies.

THEORIES AND METHODS

Some of the basis for the reform outlook was laid down through the work of the so-called Chicago school of ecological research in the 1920s. Preoccupied, perhaps in part because of their own middle-class and largely rural origins,[2] with a variety of social ills that seemed so prevalent in the modern city, these sociologists embarked on an intensive exploration of urban social structure and life styles. Utilizing a number of different investigative techniques (that ranged from the geographical mapping of various conditions and events within the city, to in-depth exploration of individual experience through the use of "personal documents" such as autobiographical essays), the Chicago researchers emphasized the intimate relation between the city's social organization and the life experiences and behavior of city-dwellers.

An important contribution of this school lay in its now classic research on juvenile delinquency. This research was based on formulations developed by Burgess, who had gone on from the concept of "natural areas" (distinctive communities within the city, each having its characteristic population composition, life styles, and problems) to analyze Chicago in terms of five concentric zones that radiated out from the central business district to the commuters' zone in the suburbs. His colleague Shaw studied officially recorded rates of juvenile delinquency and discovered a "gradient tendency" —the highest concentration of offenders' residences was in the deteriorated "zone in transition" surrounding the central business district, and rates declined progressively outward toward the suburban area.[3] Shaw and his coworkers analyzed other American cities in much the same way, and came up with similar results. Furthermore, the same general tendency was found in the distribution of other types of social "pathology"—for example, serious mental illness (as revealed through hospitalization).

Over the years this ecological approach has occasioned a great deal of controversy among sociologists. It did not take the critics long to point out the great oversimplification of ritualistically applying the specific "concentric zone" theory to all major cities. A considerable literature has also built up disputing many methodological and theoretical features of the general approach.[4] Some studies that have sought to replicate the Chicago research in other cities have tended to confirm its findings; other studies have produced data that seem to contradict those findings. Lander, using the technique of factor analysis in studying the distribution of delinquency in Baltimore, asserted that contrary to the implication of the Chicago research that delinquency was linked directly to socioeconomic status, it was instead more directly related to variables associated with the presence or absence of "anomie," in his view the percentage of owner-occupied homes in an area, and the percentage of nonwhite residents.[5] This formulation, too, has been strongly criticized on a variety of methodological grounds.[6]

Sociologists today, then, are wary of any simple generalizations based on ecological theory, but at the same time one cannot ignore the heavy concentration of officially recorded delinquency in certain areas of our large cities. Related types of youth behavior also seem to be highly concentrated in particular sections of the city. Thus Chein and his associates, in their study of juvenile drug use cited earlier, found that

> . . . juvenile drug use is not randomly distributed over New York City. It is heavily concentrated in certain neighborhoods. These are not a cross-section of the city's neighborhoods, but rather they are the ones which are economically and socially most deprived. Even within the relatively few census tracts in which we found the majority of cases, the tracts of highest drug use can be distinguished from those with lower rates of juvenile drug use by a variety of social and economic indexes. The tracts with the greatest amount of drug use are those with the highest proportions of certain minority groups, the highest poverty rates, the

most crowded dwelling units, the highest incidence of disrupted family living arrangements, and so on for a number of additional related indexes.[7]

This concentration does not imply in a simplistic way that "poverty causes delinquency"—an assertion that most sociologists would probably consider inadequate (or certainly at best incomplete). Indeed, the Chein research team explained individual differences by a family-background factor operating within the areas of high drug use. At any rate, simply to establish a statistical association between area of residence and the probability of becoming delinquent does not explain the processes by which particular individuals become delinquent. Likewise, a mapping that shows the distribution of delinquents (or delinquent acts) within a city does not constitute a "theory of delinquency." As one might expect, the Chicago sociologists were quite aware of this, and in fact devoted a good deal of effort to developing a coherent picture of the processes that lay behind the findings disclosed on their maps.

Central to these processes, they believed, were the waves of immigration and industrialization that kept certain sections of the city (particularly the "zone in transition") almost continuously disorganized—owing largely to the mobility and transiency of the residential population. Thus the high-delinquency area near the central business district was described as an "interstitial zone" in the throes of change. With perpetual change and rapid mobility, mechanisms of social control broke down, and in place of stable institutions that might promote law-abidingness, competing values (some of which encouraged delinquency and crime) emerged.[8] Although analyzing the causes of delinquency in terms of social disorganization has become quite unfashionable—partly because sociologists came to realize that in fact social life in all neighborhoods was organized, in one way or another (thus giving rise to the alternative concept of "differential social organization"), the Chicago school's focus on the neighborhood setting of delinquent behavior was extremely valuable.

This focus significantly drew attention to the role of shared values in crime and delinquency, an aspect the individual treatment outlook invariably slights. Elements of cultural conflict (between competing value systems) also were highlighted in the Chicago research. Thus in his study of over 1,300 youth gangs, Thrasher asserted that while the origins of these gangs to some extent lay in the formation of spontaneous play groups, it was disapproval by and conflict with the forces of conventional society that gave rise to group consciousness and real gang identity.[9] Above all, the work of the Chicago school documented the presence in certain urban areas of a "delinquent tradition" that might be passed on from one generation to the next. Studying delinquency rates in Chicago over time, it was found that despite continuous population shifts, wtih successive waves of immigrants replacing one another in the transitional sectors, certain areas maintained high-delinquency rates, in roughly the same proportions. The existence and cultural transmission of a delinquent tradition was even more directly demonstrated through the case histories of individual delinquents collected as part of the Chicago research. Thus "Stanley," whose autobiography was edited and interpreted by Shaw, commented:

> Stealing in the neighborhood was a common practice among the children and approved by the parents. Whenever the boys got together they talked about robbing and made more plans for stealing. I hardly knew any boys who did not go robbing. The little fellows went in for petty stealing, breaking into freight cars, and stealing junk. The older guys did big jobs like stick-up, burglary, and stealing autos. The little fellows admired the "big shots" and longed for the day when they could get into the big racket. Fellows who had "done time" were big shots and looked up to and gave the little fellows tips on how to get by and pull off big jobs.[10]

Also contributing to this "cultural transmission" perspective was Sutherland's attempt to frame a general theory of crime causation, which gave rise to the well-known sociological concept of "differential association."[11] Trying to relate the findings from traditional criminological research to his own special interests in professional theft and especially white-collar crime, Sutherland concluded that a viable crime theory would have to be formulated in terms general enough to explain every instance of crime. The usual kinds of probability statements (developed on the basis of statistical associations between standard variables) did not seem adequate. Seeking the common element in all crime, then, Sutherland realized that psychopathology or poverty would not suffice as an overall explanation, particularly for the behavior of the corporate executive white-collar criminals he studied. His general theory was basically that crime always involved learned behavior that was produced or shaped through social interaction. More specifically, the most universally applicable causal process, Sutherland claimed, was differential association: "A person becomes delinquent because of an excess of definitions favorable to violation of law over definitions unfavorable to violation of law." [12]

There has been considerable debate among sociologists as to precisely what Sutherland meant by this. Although he labeled his general principle in terms of associations, he was not simply asserting that criminals are individuals who have come into direct contact with other law-violators. While such direct association may indeed be important, Sutherland's formulation—with its reference to "definitions"—also called attention to a broader dimension of cultural attitudes and emphases that may be influential in causing delinquency. These more general cultural patterns to which individuals are exposed remain somewhat elusive, and furthermore, as Sutherland noted, they vary in "frequency, duration, priority, and intensity." Partly for this reason, researchers have found it difficult to operationalize his formulation for the purpose of testing it, although some attempts have been made. More crucially, however, some critics have insisted that by seeking a universal explanation that would cover all kinds and instances of law violation, Sutherland came up with a thesis that basically is tautological and untestable. By the same token, it is seen as an after-the-fact description of the general learning process through which all law-violatiors may have gone, but it does not provide any basis for predicting in advance just which individuals are going to become delinquents or criminals.[13] Notwithstanding these limitations, Sutherland's thesis helped to suggest the importance of learned and shared cultural aspects of crime and delinquency.

Another important strand of delinquency theory reflecting reformist assumptions focuses heavily on the criminogenic impact of the social class structure. This line of analysis derives in part from the seminal article by Merton, entitled "Social Structure and Anomie," first published in 1938.[14] Drawing on the concept of anomie (or normlessness) developed by Durkheim in his studies of the relationship between types and degrees of social cohesion and rates of suicide, Merton viewed deviant behavior—including crime and delinquency—as being generated by the social structures and cultural expectancies of the larger society within which it occurs. Such structures, Merton asserted, "exert a definite pressure upon certain persons in the society to engage in nonconforming conduct"; and this differential pressure he sought to explain through the relationship between major cultural goals ("held out as legitimate objectives for all or for diversely located members of the society") and the accepted "institutionalized" means of achieving those goals. Modes of individual adaptation, Merton argued, were determined through the various possible combinations of a person's accepting or rejecting the dominant goals and available legitimate means. Most crime and delinquency would fit under one of these possible outcomes; it would take the form of "innovation" in which the individual accepts the cultural goals but resorts to illegitimate means for their attainment. Attributing much deviance in American society to the disjunction between the heavily stressed goal of monetary success and the distribution of legitimate opportunities for achieving it, Merton stated that "It is only when a system of cultural values extols, virtually above all else, certain common success goals *for the population at large* while the social structure rigorously restricts or completely closes access to approved modes of reaching those goals *for a considerable part of the same population,* that deviant behavior ensues on a large scale."

It was partly on the foundation Merton laid down that Cohen developed his conception of the "delinquent subculture." [15] Assuming, again, that delinquency was heavily concentrated among urban lower-class youth, Cohen felt however that Merton's analysis did not do justice to the specific nature of delinquent behavior. If delinquency involved using "illicit means" to achieve common success goals, why were so many delinquent acts "nonutilitarian, malicious, and negativistic"? Cohen dealt with these qualities of "short-run hedonism" and "versatility" through the notion of collective problem-solving. Asking why a distinctive delinquent subculture had arisen, he sought to discover "those combinations of personality and situation which yield the problems of adjustment to which the delinquent subculture is an appropriate response." Following Merton's lead by focusing on the common goal of financial success, Cohen defined a broader complex of middle-class values to which, he claimed, all children in our society were subjected but in terms of which only middle-class children really could expect to succeed. Particularly in the schools, with their predominantly middle-class staff and orientations, the working-class boy was confronted with such middle-class virtues as rationality, specialization, gratification deferral, and control of aggression. Unprepared to meet these standards, he would almost certainly find himself at the bottom of the status hierarchy.

A distinctive feature of Cohen's analysis was his effort to explain the process whereby the delinquent subculture provides a solution. In his view, "These problems are chiefly status problems: certain children are denied status in the respectable society because they cannot meet the criteria of the respectable status system. The delinquent subculture deals with these problems by providing criteria of status which these children *can* meet." This occurs, Cohen argued, through a collective "reaction formation" to the middle-class values in which they are completely repudiated and an alternative value system that represents "their very antithesis" adopted. Thus, "Group stealing, institutionalized in the delinquent subculture, is not just a way of *getting* something. It is a means that is the antithesis of sober and diligent 'labor in a calling.' It expresses contempt for a way of life by making its opposite a criterion of status." [16]

Cloward and Ohlin, in their influential work, *Delinquency and Opportunity*,[17] to some extent amalgamate the perspectives emphasized in the Chicago studies and those developed by Merton and Cohen. Focusing once again on the blocked avenues for achieving success goals that working-class youth often experience (though with a heavier emphasis on economic striving than on a more general striving for status), these authors cogently stress that there are differentials in access to illegitimate means as well as to legitimate ones. As they note, this point had been at least implicit in the Chicago tradition (Sutherland, in *The Professional Thief*,[18] indicated that not only opportunity for theft, but also selection and tutelage by other thieves, were prerequisite to entering the "profession"); yet somehow it had been lost sight of in the development of an "anomie theory" of delinquency. Recognition of this factor enables them to distinguish between three major types of delinquent subculture—the criminal ("rackets" oriented) type, the conflict (or fighting gang) type, and the retreatist (or drug-oriented) type— and to suggest further the role that social structure of the local neighborhood might play in determining the particular pattern of adaptation an individual might be most likely to adopt.

According to Cloward and Ohlin, delinquent responses vary from one neighborhood to another, depending primarily on the "integration of different age-levels of offenders" and the "integration of conventional and deviant values." The criminal type of adaptation, for example, requires

> . . . a neighborhood milieu characterized by close bonds between different age-levels of offenders, and between criminal and conventional elements. As a consequence of these integrative relationships, a new opportunity structure emerges which provides alternative avenues to success-goals. Hence the pressures generated by restrictions on legitimate access to success-goals are drained off. Social controls over the conduct of the young are effectively exercised, limiting expressive behavior and constraining the discontented to adopt instrumental, if criminalistic, styles of life.[19]

Not all slum neighborhoods, however, are sufficiently stable and well-integrated to provide an alternative avenue to success; in the more truly disorganized slum, where there is not only lack of access to legitimate opportunities but also no base for "stable criminal opportunity systems," the stage is well set for the violent behavior of the conflict subculture. Cloward and Ohlin do not delineate quite as clearly the structural sources of the third type of adaptation, the drug-oriented subculture, which they assert may draw youths who are "double failures." For those youths who "have failed to find a place for themselves in criminal or conflict subcultures," the drug-oriented way of life may have a special appeal.

The formulations of Merton, Cohen, and Cloward and Ohlin all have been subjected to numerous lines of criticism.[20] One of the strongest of the criticisms has attacked the apparent assumption that delinquency is primarily a working-class phenomenon, and the analytic preoccupation of these authors with the delinquencies of working-class youth. We shall return to this issue in Chapter Five. Critics also assert that these theorists have made questionable assumptions regarding the nature of working-class aspirations and feelings, and the relationship between such aspirations and the likelihood of engaging in delinquent behavior. Clearly the specific theories differ from one another in various respects, but certain common features mark them (together with the ecological studies and Sutherland's work) as fitting in with the liberal reform response. As we have seen, they all direct our attention to aspects of the sociocultural context of delinquency—to the group setting and the role of peers, to neighborhood traditions and social structures, and to the impact on the individual of his position in the social class order. Furthermore, they all assume that certain individuals are in one way or another constrained to violate the law, another major point of contention to which we shall return below.

A rather different kind of formulation in some ways is Miller's thesis that delinquent behavior directly reflects the norms of lower-class culture: "In the case of 'gang' delinquency, the cultural system which exerts the most direct influence on behavior is that of the lower-class community itself—a long-established, distinctively patterned tradition with an integrity of its own—rather than a so-called 'delinquent subculture' which has arisen through conflict with middle-class culture and is oriented to the deliberate violation of middle-class norms." [21] According to Miller, urban lower-class life possesses a set of distinctive "focal concerns" ("areas or issues which command widespread and persistent attention and a high degree of emotional involvement"), some of which directly or indirectly promote violation of middle-class laws. The major focal concerns are: *trouble* (in some situations "getting into trouble" may be acceptable as a means to a desired goal, and it may even confer prestige); *tough-*

ness (an "almost obsessive" concern with masculinity which Miller, interestingly, sees as a reaction-formation to a predominantly female-based household—an analysis Parsons and Cohen, it will be recalled, used to explain middle-class delinquency); *smartness* (the capacity to outsmart others, and not be "taken" oneself); *excitement* (adventure and the search for thrills, which may be counterbalanced however by periods of inactivity such as "hanging out"); *fate* (belief that one's life is subject to forces beyond one's control, which may lead to a belief that rational goal-seeking is futile); and *autonomy* (overt resentment of external control, which may be coupled however with covert desire for nurturance and "authority").

Miller makes much of the female-based household (the prevalence and effects of which, actually, are matters of considerable dispute) and concludes that the "one-sex peer unit" becomes particularly important because it satisfies needs for "belonging" and "status" not provided by the family. Positive efforts to satisfy these needs and desires and to achieve goals through culturally prescribed (i.e., lower-class) means, are what lead lower-class youths into law violations, not some complicated psychological reaction to middle-class standards. In this connection, Miller interestingly suggests that since much lower-class behavior patently violates middle-class norms, predominantly middle-class observers have simply assumed (unwarrantedly, he believes) that the motivation for such behavior has to involve some reaction to middle-class standards. However, he contends:

> No cultural pattern as well-established as the practice of illegal acts by members of lower-class corner groups could persist if buttressed primarily by negative, hostile, or rejective motives; its principal motivational support, as in the case of any persisting cultural tradition, derives from a positive effort to achieve what is valued within that tradition and to conform to its explicit and implicit norms.[22]

Needless to say, Miller's formulation has occasioned a good deal of controversy. For one thing, if his thesis is accurate then virtually all urban lower-class youth should, almost by definition, be delinquent. Yet we know that this is not so. Furthermore, while as an anthropologist Miller meant to simply describe and interpret cultural patterns in a disinterested nonethnocentric way (and indeed to emphasize that these patterns have their own "integrity"), his findings certainly could be used by political and social conservatives to conclude that the poor are basically no good. Finally, critics question his thesis regarding the nature of dominant lower-class values; as we shall see further, sociologists disagree on the issue of whether working-class youths reject or accept the dominant middle-class values, and this has compounded the problem of understanding the precise motivation underlying lower-class delinquency.

STREET-GANG WORK

As one would expect, those who believe that delinquency is best understood in terms of peer influences, neighborhood, and social class will try to effect changes in these elements. The community itself, rather than specified individuals, comes to be seen as requiring "treatment." Such treatment takes a number of forms. One of the most common involves efforts by "street workers," "gang workers," or "detached workers" (as they are alternatively called) to steer the behavior of gang members into acceptable channels. Although the term "gang" is often used loosely, and the criminal activity of gangs sometimes exaggerated, without doubt there are a good many youth groups (varying however in degree of organization and extent of criminal involvement) that do sometimes engage in behavior that the public would understandably be concerned about.

A leading gang specialist has described street work with gangs as follows:

> Although varying in form, detached work programs are grounded in one basic proposition: Because gang members do not ordinarily respond well to standard agency programs inside the agency walls, it is necessary to take the programs to the gangs. Around this simple base of a worker reaching out to his client, other programmatic thrusts then take form—club meetings, sports activities, tutoring and remedial reading projects, leader-

ship training, family counseling, casework, employment training, job finding, and so on. In addition, a community organization component is often built into the program in recognition that gangs do not exist in a vacuum, but in a context permeated by adults and adult organization.[23]

As this statement suggests, gang work actually may incorporate some treatment aspects, and particular programs will vary considerably in their emphasis on the community. However, most of these programs do imply a recognition (by "reaching out" to the client) of the importance of groups and the community context, even in dealing with problems of specific individuals within gangs.

The street worker's central problem is achieving rapport with gang members. Members of the gang should not view the "detached" worker as being too closely identified with formal agencies —particularly official agencies of social control, like the police. Even voluntary social agencies, especially to the extent they have been staffed by nonresidents of the local community, are suspect. In order to ease the difficulties of attaining rapport, older youths or young adults indigenous to the community have often been sought as street workers. The worker must at one and the same time convince the gang members he is "on their side" and yet not indicate approval of all their behavior. Somehow the goal of influencing the gang must be reconciled with that of providing friendly help and support. This task is rendered especially difficult because the worker tries to provide a service for those who have not sought his help, and he has to do this in an unstructured, highly fluid context, within which he has relatively little direct control over his working conditions.[24] Some street workers have managed to develop remarkable rapport with gang members and at the same time avoid cooptation. While the worker should exploit the rapport he has developed to "cool" gang fights and deter members from criminal acts, he may have to contact the police if such efforts are unsuccessful. Apparently, if this policy is made quite explicit, gang members can accept it and yet not necessarily distrust or reject the street worker.

While specific programs differ as to guidelines for street workers, the need for flexibility in facing complex and continuously changing situations generally dictates a policy of allowing the workers considerable freedom to adopt their own distinctive styles of work and deal with incidents "on the spot" more or less according to their best personal judgment. As a consequence, one finds a variety of modes of operation in street-gang work; and whereas one particular style may prove effective in some ways and in some situations, a quite different approach may be equally useful under another set of conditions. A report on street workers who participated in the Midcity Youth Project refers to five distinct styles of work, which its authors suggestively describe in the following terms: the "professional," the "ideologist," the "moralist," the "socializer," and the "manipulator." [25] Excerpts from that account show that the worker may not only adopt a distinctive everyday work style, but may also selectively pursue particular goals in line with his general orientations to delinquency problems and to his own work with gangs. This is evident in some of the comments about M (a "professional") and H (a "manipulator").

> He [M] adhered to the belief that an individual's maturation may be promoted by participation in organized groups guided by trained personnel. Therefore he strove always to keep his personal influence minimal so that major decisions would come from the boys themselves. He did not attempt to alter their status or make them upwardly mobile or impose upon them a proletarian piety, but cultivated the traditions of the gang itself and its neighborhood to fortify their feeling for their own small community.

> M's orientation, which we call *civicism*, was in general conservative, aimed at the integration of disengaged youth into the mainstream of indigenous culture. Ultimately, he was trying to fashion a movement that would include both adults and the gangs. In many respects, then, he was a traditionalist: the Outlaws and similar organized youths, he felt, should endure. He was apt to ignore the fact that in Midcity there was no traditional neighborhood organization of the kind he sought and no tradition of youth movements with civic or other social commitments. Undaunted, he bent his efforts toward providing the gang an ideology counter to its own, while the neighborhood, he hoped, would eventually organize to solve its own problems, including those of its young people.[26]

Professionally trained in group work, H engaged in extensive maneuvering and manipulation to keep his gang out of trouble and develop law-abiding activities for its members.

> He showed none of the professional's visionariness and doctrinal commitment but much of the practical man's scorn of intellectualism and Utopianism. He liked to manipulate institutions on behalf of his boys, since beyond the practical value of his masterful strategies was his private enjoyment of the political process itself. He appeared to know instinctively that, as a gang worker, one of his most significant functions was to bridge the gap between the corner institution and the political and social structure of Midcity, a gap created as the power and importance of local politicians declined with the growth of the national welfare system. . . .
>
> To H, an individual's rise to greater occupational prestige was good, and everything possible should be done to encourage personal ambition. He was passionately opposed to economic or political discrimination. In principle, he sought the complete conversion of both aspiring and unaspiring boys but was reluctant to engage in the arduous labor of stirring up the unambitious. He tended, then, to attract boys whose families had inculcated in them ambitions for a college education and mobility generally.[27]

Whatever specific emphasis the street worker chooses to adopt, it will take some time before his influence begins to be felt, and many of the manifestations of this influence will be subtle and long-term ones. One does not simply step into a gang situation, obtain immediate acceptance, and start changing things. On the contrary, gang work usually involves a considerable period of general exploration, initial contacting and mutual "testing," out of which may come an informal working agreement on the nature and extent of the worker-gang relationship.[28] It is only after these stages of the street-work process have been completed that the worker can realistically hope to begin to have an impact. And the nature of the impact is highly variable. Most dramatic of course, and likely to receive the most publicity, are those instances in which the worker manages to prevent an impending violent confrontation between

fighting gangs. But as we have seen the extent of sheer gang violence, particularly of this organized sort, has often been exaggerated.
There are, too, a great many specific ways in which the worker can
assist the gang and individual members—some of which were noted
above. Perhaps one of the most important kinds of impact the
worker may have lies in the vital but more elusive area of general
attitudes. As Austin has properly noted:

> By his behavior he seeks to break down certain stereotypes the
> group has created about adults which form a convenient ra-
> tionale for much of their attitude and behavior. This stereotype
> is that adults are against us, they don't understand us, if they
> pretend to be interested in us it is for their own purposes, and
> even if they are really sympathetic with us they are inconsistent
> and undependable. To the degree that the worker is successful in
> refuting these stereotypes through his own behavior, he opens
> the door for possible communication between himself and the
> group members and ultimately between the group members and
> other adults.[29]

At the same time, and on a more specific level, he may provide a
socially acceptable "role model" with which many of the youths
may choose to identify.

When one considers the intangible nature of some of these
goals, it is easy to see why evaluation of street-work programs is
extremely difficult. Even with more specific and more readily
measurable aims, the free-wheeling and highly variable nature of
street work prevents the accurate and uniform recording of necessary data. Recently researchers have begun to face this problem;
it has been suggested that relatively simple standard procedures
might be developed to collect much useful information for com-
puterized storage, retrieval, and eventual analysis.[30] The evaluation of the present programs—by more traditional methods and by
the usual criteria for success in reducing delinquency—has not
shown them to be very effective. Indeed, according to one recent
appraisal, they "have proven only slightly successful, ineffective,
or even contributory to gang delinquency. They have employed
inadequate resources in combating an entrenched foe. Some of their

normal and almost necessary practices have acted as boomerangs, effectively increasing gang cohesiveness and delinquency." [31]

This statement suggests a persistent underlying issue in street work—whether, while seeking to encourage socially acceptable behavior patterns among the members, one should try to strengthen the group or instead try to dissolve it. Uncertainty on this point reflects the evident lack of consensus regarding the nature of "gangs"; some observers view these groups as typically being well-organized and serving important functions for their members, and others see them as much more loosely structured and considerably less significant for the members. One major analyst of gang work, Klein, insists that it is a major error to view the gang as a "natural" group that should be reinforced or strengthened. On the basis of his experience with several programs in Los Angeles, he contends that the ultimate goal of street work should be

> . . . group *dissolution* through counteracting those factors which bring about group cohesiveness. The juvenile gang, I hasten to add, is one of the very few social problem aggregates for which such an approach is appropriate. We have found individual counseling to be relatively fruitless. The same is true of efforts at community organization or the modification of agency policies. The target should be group dissolution by discouraging group activities as such and by identification and provision of a variety of nongang alternatives.[32]

Concluding that "one successful job experience is worth months of intensive counseling," Klein and his associates embarked on a project that emphasized employment to reduce gang cohesiveness and therefore delinquency as well. They found that these efforts had a distinct impact on group cohesiveness; and although this did not lead to a lower delinquency *rate* (ratio of offenses to gang members), the absolute number of offenses was distinctly reduced. An important factor that led to this result, they assert, was that "gang recruitment ceased completely during the project. Thus, as boys grew older and conributed less to juvenile arrests, they were not replaced by younger members . . . in sufficient numbers to maintain the original group level of offenses." [33] Some of the difficulties that confront efforts to emphasize job-finding are suggested, however, in another report, this one on a gang program in Chicago: "about 78 percent of the jobs obtained have been lost, with 'fired,' 'quit,' and 'laid off' accounting for roughly equal proportions. . . . The average length of employment was three months, and the most frequently given reason for loss of job was absenteeism." [34]

One of the most ambitious programs involving street-gang work was the Midcity Youth Project, referred to above. This was an action-research "demonstration project" conducted in the Roxbury district of Boston between 1954 and 1957. Although it has been described as a "total community" approach,[35] the core of the program was field work with gangs. During the three-year period, seven street workers maintained contact with approximately 400 members of some twenty-one corner gangs; more intensive work was undertaken with seven of these gangs (around 200 members). Methods employed by the individual street workers varied a good deal. Services provided by the workers covered the full range of possibilities already mentioned. According to Miller, the project was quite successful in changing informal gangs into clubs or athletic teams (which could then engage in appropriate and legitimate activities), in providing job guidance and placement assistance, and generally in serving as intermediary between the gang members and various local institutions.

> . . . as a consequence of the workers' activities, gang members gained access to a wide variety of legitimate adult institutions and organizations—schools, business establishments, settlement houses, municipal athletic leagues, public recreational facilities, guidance services, health facilities, municipal governmental agencies, citizens groups, and others. It could no longer be said that the groups were isolated, in any practical sense, from the world of legitimate opportunity.[36]

Especially interesting from our standpoint, as a reflection of the persistence of treatment outlooks and the attempt to combine them with community perspectives, are the same author's comments regarding efforts to "induce personality change." As he points out, most of the project's workers had received training in psychodynamic therapy principles, and considerable thought was given to applying these principles as a formal part of the program. However, "after much discussion workers decided that the use of techniques appropriate to the controlled therapist-patient situation would not be practicable in the open and multi-cliented arena of the corner gang world. . . ." [37] Therefore it was decided to employ psychotherapeutic approaches only indirectly, through close consultation with psychiatrists at a local child-guidance clinic, and through "group dynamics" techniques during various kinds of meetings with gang members. Yet Miller concludes that from the standpoint of "personality change," the most effective device was simply "the continued presence with the group of a law-abiding, middle-class-oriented adult who provided active support for a particular value position." [38] There were clear indications in the course of the project that the "role model" potential of street workers can be an extremely strong and constructive one.

Unfortunately, the apparent success in these areas was not accompanied by reduced delinquency. Miller states:

> It is now possible to provide a definite answer to the principal evaluative research question—"Was there a significant measurable inhibition of law-violating or morally disapproved behavior as a consequence of Project efforts?" The answer, with little necessary qualification, is "No." All major measures of violative behavior—disapproved actions, illegal actions, during-contact court appearances, before-during-after appearances, and Project-Control group appearances—provide consistent support for a finding of "negligible impact." [39]

Since the Project employed in varying degrees a large number of different methods all aimed at reducing delinquency—ranging from community organization efforts to family therapy—it is difficult to determine just which of these techniques achieved relative success and which did not. Some of the methods, such as "effecting concerted effort between citizens' groups and professional agencies, and coordinating the varied efforts of professional agencies themselves," were not carried out sufficiently to provide a reasonable test of their efficacy.

COMMUNITY ACTION PROGRAMS

Of the programs that have adopted a more thoroughgoing "total community" approach to delinquency prevention, two are perhaps best known—Mobilization for Youth, in New York City, and the Chicago Area Project. The former, explicitly grounded in Cloward and Ohlin's "opportunity" theory, has been described as

> . . . an *integrated* approach to the environmental system which in our view produces delinquency. . . . It is our belief that delinquent behavior is engendered because *opportunities for conformity are limited*—that the desire to meet social expectations itself becomes the source of delinquent behavior if the possibility of doing so is limited or nonexistent. If we wish to reduce the incidence of delinquent behavior or rehabilitate those already so engaged, we must provide the social and psychological resources that make conformity possible.[40]

Serving New York's Lower East Side, a racially and ethnically heterogeneous area "with a long and colorful tradition presenting the assets, the problems, and the weaknesses of a complex high density, low income, urban community," Mobilization has offered an extremely wide range of programs and services. The positive note struck in the "opportunities" focus is seen in efforts to *create new* employment opportunities, and in community organization aimed at *direct action* on other aspects of the poverty situation to actively promote social change. Thus development of tenants' organizations, voter registration campaigns, concerted tutoring efforts, provision of legal services, and the like, are emphasized more than conventional agency functions. The rationale for such measures is quite explicit:

> We equate unaffiliation with powerlessness, and lack of power plays a crucial role in the inability of the slum community to help itself. With all the services being brought to bear on the slum community . . . we believe this is not enough. Something must be done to help the adult community achieve adequate in-

stitutional connections, because it is through these connections that adults can play a role in affecting necessary community change. Participation, then, is the key here.[41]

We shall return later to this important issue of participation and power. Another distinctive aspect of this approach is that in a program like that of Mobilization for Youth, efforts to reduce delinquency are not exclusively aimed at delinquent youths themselves. Particularly significant is the notion that one way of preventing delinquency is to increase the community power of adults, and hence indirectly through general social change to affect the lives of children.

A forerunner of the Mobilization project, and indeed the prototype of all community delinquency programs, the Chicago Area Project arose in connection with the early urban research of Shaw and his associates. Heavily grounded in the theoretical assumptions of that research, the Project's main goal was to promote social change at the neighborhood level; a desire for change on the part of community residents, and a sense of meaningful participation in program efforts were seen as vitally necessary ingredients for such change. Indeed, the Chicago Project's well-formulated orienting thesis provided the groundwork for Mobilization and similar recent programs:

> The organized activity of people everywhere flows in the channels of institutions and organizations indigenous to their cultural traditions and to the system of social relationships which defines their social groups. Consequently one could not expect people to devote their energies to enterprises which form part of the social systems of groups in which they have no membership. . . . There had always existed an expectation that people residing in the high-delinquency rate areas could somehow be induced to support the welfare agencies there. A basic assumption of the Area Project program was that under prevailing conditions it was illusory to expect this to happen.[42]

In line with these assumptions, the major strategy of the Project was to organize community residents into many committees through which welfare programs could be developed and administered.

Here again, there was a wide range of specific services offered.

Spokesmen for the Project claim that the effort to tap and rely on indigenous leadership has largely been successful. "Even in the most unlikely localities capable persons of good will have responded to the challenge of responsibility and have, with help and guidance, operated neighborhood programs. On the whole these organizations have exhibited vitality and stability and have come to represent centers of local opinion regarding issues which concern the welfare of the young." [43] Some statistics suggest that delinquency rates declined in areas served by the Project; but as one commentator has noted, this evidence did not stem from controlled comparisons and must therefore be considered inconclusive.[44] Generally speaking, there has been little systematic evaluation of community organization programs of this sort; and where this has occurred (as in the Midcity Youth Project) the results have been discouraging. Nonetheless, the strategy of organizing and employing local community resources, and expanding opportunities is currently looked on with considerable favor in crime control and prevention circles.

Community organization efforts clearly raise special problems of interinstitutional cooperation, and as recent controversies regarding the organization of school systems indicate, the issue of "community control" has potent political implications. In a later section, we shall consider various "political" aspects of delinquency problems. As for the expansion of opportunities, local employment efforts and educational assistance programs are now especially likely to receive support. We have seen that programs to provide jobs for slum youths are not always smooth-running; furthermore, the exact relationship between employment and delinquency remains unclear. Nonetheless, several studies have suggested that high-employment and low-delinquency rates are closely associated,[45] and we can probably expect that delinquency-prevention programs will take advantage of this possible link. Reform-oriented educational programs at the local level have focused heavily on the improvement of school facilities and the provision of preparatory, guidance, and "compensatory" services for preschool and school children. As we shall see, critics more and more are insisting

that such measures—however commendable—often deflect attention from the core problems of our educational system that may
have a greater bearing on delinquency.

GENERAL SOCIAL REFORM

The reform impulse in delinquency policy extends well beyond
these community efforts. For one thing, with growing public concern and increased federal funding, programs in job training and
placement, community organization, and even street-gang work to
an extent have become aspects of national policy. As such, they
may be strengthened at the local levels through the added support,
guidance, and coordination provided by federal agencies; or they
may be hampered by the doctrinal and bureaucratic rigidities that
often characterize these agencies. Invariably, in developing co-
ordinated preventive programs, agencies will adopt a particular
stance toward the clients and the "problem." By and large, programs that are "community based," that involve local "participation," and that aim at expanding legitimate "opportunities" are
especially in favor at the present time; and these programs most
directly reflect the assumptions of liberal reform.

A related, but somewhat different, policy perspective sees the
most promising line of attack on delinquency not in socially oriented
delinquency programs, but in more general social reform. According to this view, a reduction in delinquency is most likely to occur
as an *indirect* consequence of much broader social and economic
change. This was a major theme in the reports of the President's
Crime Commission, which noted: "The underlying problems are
ones that the criminal justice system can do little about. . . . Unless society does take concerted action to change the general conditions and attitudes that are associated with crime, no improvement in law enforcement and administration of justice, the subjects
this Commission was specifically asked to study, will be of much
avail." [46]

From this standpoint, the root causes of delinquency are socioeconomic inequality, racism, and widely prevalent criminogenic

value systems. Direct and meaningful measures to eliminate or reduce poverty, inequality of opportunity, and associated living conditions are seen to have a particularly strong potential for ultimately reducing crime and delinquency.[47] To the professional sociologist, this line of argument presents several difficulties. As a formal causal explanation that is both theoretically grounded and empirically testable, the assertion that poverty causes crime or delinquency is not really acceptable. It clearly does not explain why some of the poor become delinquent and others do not. Then too, as we have seen (and further documentation is provided below), sociologists increasingly question the assumption that usually underlies this thesis—namely, that delinquency is heavily concentrated in the working or lower-class segments of the population. But even if these limitations could be disregarded, simply to attribute delinquency to poverty would in no way indicate the specific processes that produce it.

Notwithstanding these problems, most sociological students of delinquency probably would applaud an all-out "war on poverty" as an important step in reducing youthful misbehavior. To some extent, they tend toward an ideological disposition favoring general amelioration of prevailing socioeconomic conditions. Furthermore, many sociologists do continue to believe that most serious delinquency is concentrated in the working-class sector. Many of them still view poverty as a root causal condition—whatever intervening processes may also be involved in the emergence of delinquent behavior among particular individuals. Even those who now contend that delinquency is not necessarily more common among the lower classes than the middle classes, consider antipoverty policies an important step in reducing the large amount of lower-class delinquency that unquestionably does exist—whatever additional policies might also be called for.

General socioeconomic reform suggests a potential point of contact between the liberal reformist position and a more radical stance on delinquency problems. These policies could produce a broad and dramatic restructuring of the socioeconomic order, and obviously go beyond what is ordinarily implied by the liberal reform perspective. The distinction, however, between "piecemeal reform" and "structural change" is a matter of degree. Certainly there is the potential for a relatively smooth passage from one to the other. But a truly radical position on delinquency involves other areas besides socioeconomic change, and there are strong tendencies working against broadly radical measures.

Most significant, reform policies persist in focusing on supposedly distinctive troublemaking individuals. This approach has been most cogently described as "blaming the victim," and its spirit is succinctly captured in the following passage by William Ryan:

> The new ideology attributes defect and inadequacy to the malignant nature of poverty, injustice, slum life, and racial difficulties. The stigma that marks the victim and accounts for his victimization is an acquired stigma, a stigma of social, rather than genetic, origin. But the stigma, the defect, the fatal difference—though derived in the past from environmental forces—is still located *within* the victim, inside his skin. With such an elegant formulation, the humanitarian can have it both ways. He can, all at the same time, concentrate his charitable interest on the defects of the victim, condemn the vague social and environmental stresses that produced the defect (some time ago), and ignore the continuing effect of victimizing social forces (right now). It is a brilliant ideology for justifying a perverse form of social action designed to change, not society, as one might expect, but rather society's victim.[48]

Although Ryan had in mind a broad spectrum of social welfare programs and attitudes, his formulation is especially enlightening with respect to juvenile justice. Victim-blaming is, as he so rightly emphasizes, a mechanism admirably suited to accommodating the tenacious hold of treatment perspectives on the public and even the professional consciousness. Paternalistic and patronizing charitable impulses have, from the beginning, characterized the juvenile court movement. Of course, the rationale for this lay in the notion of the child's dependency, of the need for the court to intervene in the child's alleged interest; yet we know that this rationale has been pushed well beyond the situation of young children in clear need of protection or supervision. Reform policies, and the sociological theories underlying them, continue this paternalism even as the earlier stress on personal pathology is ostensibly abandoned. The very term "juvenile"—an almost entirely legal designation, often quite inappropriate to the maturity and situation of youthful offenders—illustrates this. So do such notions as "culturally deprived" and "culturally disadvantaged," which derive from reform-oriented research and which continue to place the focus on the individual.

Part of what is involved here is the aforementioned "evil causes evil" fallacy. Our inability to designate specific "bad" conditions that generate delinquent behavior seems to remain unacceptable. Yet apparently there are distinct limits on the extent to which we are willing to uncompromisingly indict our social structures and approved value systems. An early text, in some ways extremely radical for the time, was titled *The Juvenile in Delinquent Society*.[49] It is not surprising that the full implications of this idea are invariably resisted, even under ideologies that favor social amelioration. This is most intriguingly illustrated by the Soviet Union's experience with delinquency problems. Under the influence of Marxist ideology, according to which delinquency and other capitalist social problems should disappear with the advent of socialism, Soviet officials are extremely hard put to explain the persistence of youthful deviance. On the one hand, they are committed to extreme notions of social (especially economic) determinism, and on the other hand they can hardly attribute offending behavior to the very socialist conditions under which the basic goodness of man is supposed to be revealed. As Walter Connor has recently shown in an excellent analysis of Soviet deviance policies, one way out of this dilemma is to focus on the alleged malfunctioning of specific institutions, on identifiable and remediable failures to achieve the standards of a socialist society. Connor notes that this strand of Soviet thought

> . . . seeks the sources of delinquency in the failure of various concrete social institutions, such as the family, school, factory, and youth organization, to socialize and control youth. Prevention of delinquency is thus primarily a matter of increasing the effectiveness of these institutions. Such an approach involves, essentially, a denial that there are delinquency-provoking factors

inherent in Soviet society and also denies that the delinquent is, *ab ovo*, a special type of person (he is made, not born). It seeks explanations in the workings of the infrastructure of Soviet society. Thus, it maintains ideological acceptability while admitting, as a practical matter, that the performances of concrete institutions of control and socialization both can be and are frequently flawed.[50]

The reformist stance confronts even more dilemmas in the area of cultural value change than in that of socioeconomic reform. Cultural values are central to many of the major theories of delinquency causation—as seen for example in Merton's focus on "success goals" and Sutherland's more general "definitions" that promote or inhibit law-violation. Again, as in the case of poverty, sociologists tend to reject a straightforward assertion that the approved values of our society "cause" crime; indeed, the Merton and Sutherland formulations suggest conditions under which this association may occur. Yet a focus on reordering cultural values could provide the basis for policies to produce quite radical changes in the "quality of life" and in attitudes. Intentional value change is notoriously difficult to produce, but broad policies could be designed to influence values—for example, in the schools and in advertising and marketing practices, rather than simply through such traditional vehicles as religious training. That this has not occurred is partly attributable to the built-in timidity of the liberal reform outlook. It may be true that the mass media primarily reinforce already existing values, rather than create new ones, but most of the research on which this conclusion is based has examined the short-run effects of attempts to change specific attitudes. We know little about the long-term subtle effects of the media on general values that may have a bearing on crime and delinquency.[51]

Typically, the liberal reformer approaches this area with an eye to very narrow policy applications. He may, for example, favor control over crime comics and television violence instead of control over the media's reinforcement of "commodity consciousness." In the former case, even though the empirical evidence that links television violence to deviance is inconclusive if not negative, the belief in the existence of this connection is consistent with the differentiating and compartmentalizing preferences discussed earlier. Policies specifically aimed at delinquency may continue, in this outlook, to receive automatic preference over policies that would only indirectly influence delinquent behavior. The reformist can also evade the issue of major cultural change by differentiating and localizing the values said to be conducive to delinquency. Thus he can claim that American values do not generally breed youth crime, but rather it is caused by the distinctive values of the "delinquent subculture" or of "lower-class culture" itself (although Cohen saw the dominant values of our society crucially implicated in the sub-cultural system). As we shall see, a general critique of prevailing values is part of the recent trend toward policies that go well beyond the assumptions of the liberal reform model.

SOCIALIZED JUSTICE

Reform assumptions and theories on the administration of juvenile justice need not differ greatly from those of the treatment perspective. Reformists will not necessarily advocate altering the traditionally broad jurisdiction of the juvenile court. They regard an extremely broad range of young people as being susceptible to trouble—an even broader range really than that cited by individual treatment proponents. Skeptical of the psychologically oriented attempts to identify in advance individual predelinquents, and also favorably disposed to preventive programs that take into account social context, the reformist nonetheless still believes that the court may steer kids in need of help into the proper channels. Similarly, the reformist will not always object to the procedural laxity of the juvenile court, and its emphasis on a broad investigation of the youth's problems and prospects, even though he might say the inquiry should be predominantly social rather than psychiatric.

Again, while the reformist favors community-based programs, he would not necessarily advocate abolishing efforts to rehabilitate individuals. All such efforts, he would argue, should reflect aware-ness of the social context in which the delinquency developed. Juvenile justice personnel should be given better training, especially in social science, and greater job incentives should be provided to attract more highly qualified individuals. Facilities should be improved, and caseloads (as in probation) lightened. In short, the reformist considers the overall system worth keeping—indeed in some ways it should be strengthened—but it should be given a broader sociocultural focus.

The continuity between the individual treatment and reformist patterns is seen especially in the persistence in one form or another of the "rehabilitative ideal." Whether the focus is on the individual psyche, the neighborhood or the peer group, policy remains directed toward treating pathological conditions believed to "cause" delinquency. And it is assumed that such policies will do more good than harm. Finally, neither the assignment of individual responsibility for particular offending acts, nor the questionably broad scope of delinquency laws themselves, is a central concern to the reformists. However, the reformist model is increasingly coming under attack. But before turning to our third reaction pattern, in which almost all of these assumptions and preferences are challenged, we should consider a number of important general developments in the analysis of deviance and social control. They have played an important role in laying the groundwork for the radical noninterventionist position.

✠   ✠   ✠

1. David Matza, *Delinquency and Drift* (New York: John Wiley & Sons, Inc., 1964), p. 17.

2. See C. Wright Mills, "The Professional Ideology of Social Pathologists," *American Journal of Sociology*, 49 (September, 1943), 165–80.

3. Clifford R. Shaw, *Delinquency Areas* (Chicago: University of Chicago Press, 1929); Shaw, Henry D. McKay, et al., *Juvenile Delinquency and Urban Areas* (Chicago: University of Chicago Press, 1942).

4. For a general discussion of the Chicago approach, see Terence Morris, *The Criminal Area* (London: Routledge & Kegan Paul, Ltd., 1958). A good recent discussion of methodological issues is Robert A. Gordon, "Issues in the Ecological Study of Delinquency," *American Sociological Review*, 32 (December, 1967), 927–44.

5. Bernard Lander, *Towards an Understanding of Juvenile Delinquency* (New York: Columbia University Press, 1954).

6. Gordon, "Issues in the Ecological Study of Delinquency."

7. Isidor Chein, et al., *The Road to H: Narcotics, Delinquency, and Social Policy* (New York: Basic Books, Inc., 1964), p. 78.

8. See Solomon Kobrin, "The Conflict of Values in Delinquency Areas," *American Sociological Review*, 16 (October, 1951), 653–61.

9. Frederic M. Thrasher, *The Gang* (Chicago: University of Chicago Press, 1927).

10. Clifford R. Shaw, *The Jack-Roller: A Delinquent Boy's Own Story*, Phoenix Books (Chicago: University of Chicago Press, 1930, 1966), p. 54.

11. See Edwin H. Sutherland and Donald R. Cressey, *Principles of Criminology*, 8th ed. (Philadelphia: J. B. Lippincott Co., 1970), pp. 75–77; also Albert K. Cohen, Alfred R. Lindesmith, and Karl Schuessler, eds., *The Sutherland Papers* (Bloomington: Indiana University Press, 1956).

12. *Ibid.*

13. See, for example, Ralph H. Turner, "The Quest for Universals in Sociological Research," *American Sociological Review*, 18 (1953), 604–611; also Travis Hirschi, *Causes of Delinquency* (Berkeley: University of California Press, 1969), pp. 13–15.

14. Robert K. Merton, "Social Structure and Anomie," *American Sociological Review*, 3 (October, 1938), 672–82; revised and expanded in Merton, *Social Theory and Social Structure*, rev. ed. (New York: Free Press, 1957).

15. Albert K. Cohen, *Delinquent Boys: The Culture of the Gang* (New York: Free Press, 1955).

16. *Ibid.*, pp. 121, 134.

17. Richard A. Cloward and Lloyd E. Ohlin, *Delinquency and Opportunity: A Theory of Delinquent Gangs* (New York: Free Press, 1960).

18. *The Professional Thief—By a Professional Thief*, annotated and interpreted by Edwin H. Sutherland, Phoenix Books (Chicago: University of Chicago Press, 1937, 1956).

19. Cloward and Ohlin, *Delinquency and Opportunity*, p. 171.

20. See Hirschi, *Causes of Delinquency*, pp. 4–10; also David J. Bordua, "A Critique of Sociological Interpretations of Gang Delinquency," *Annals of the American Academy of Political and Social Science*, 338 (November, 1961), 120–36.

21. Walter P. Miller, "Lower Class Culture as a Generating Milieu of Gang Delinquency," *Journal of Social Issues*, 14 (Summer, 1958), 5–19; as reprinted in James F. Short, Jr., ed., *Gang Delinquency and Delinquent Subcultures* (New York: Harper & Row, Publishers, 1968), p. 136.

22. *Ibid.*, p. 156.

23. Malcolm W. Klein, *Street Gangs and Street Workers* (Englewood Cliffs, N.J.: Prentice-Hall, Inc., 1971), p. 46.

24. See David M. Austin, "Goals for Gang Workers," in Stratton and Terry, *Prevention of Delinquency* (New York: The Macmillan Company, 1968), pp. 255–65.

25. David Kanter and William Ira Bennett, "Orientations of Street-Corner Workers and their Effect on Gangs," in Stanton Wheeler, ed., *Controlling Delinquents* (New York: John Wiley & Sons, Inc., 1968), pp. 271–86.

26. *Ibid.*, pp. 280–81.

27. *Ibid.*, p. 284.

28. Austin, "Goals for Gang Workers," p. 261.

29. *Ibid.*, p. 262.

30. Hugh F. Cline, Howard E. Freeman, and Stanton Wheeler, "The Analysis and Evaluation of Detached-Worker Programs," in Wheeler, ed., *Controlling Delinquents*, pp. 287–315.

31. Klein, *Street Gangs and Street Workers*, p. 55.

32. *Ibid.*, p. 234.

33. *Ibid.*, p. 304.

34. Charles N. Cooper, "The Chicago YMCA Detached Workers: Current Status of an Action Program," in Klein, *Juvenile Gangs in Context* (Englewood Cliffs, N.J.: Prentice-Hall, 1967), p. 191.

35. Walter P. Miller, "The Impact of a 'Total-Community' Delinquency Control Project," *Social Problems*, 10 (Fall, 1962), 168–91; as reprinted in Rose Giallombardo, ed., *Juvenile Delinquency* (New York: John Wiley & Sons, Inc., 1966), pp. 493–516.

36. *Ibid.*, p. 498.

37. *Ibid.*, p. 499.

38. *Ibid.*

39. *Ibid.*, p. 512.

40. Marylyn Bibb, "Gang-Related Services of Mobilization for Youth," in Klein, *Juvenile Gangs in Context*, p. 176.

41. *Ibid.*, p. 181.

42. Solomon Kobrin, "The Chicago Area Project—A 25-Year Assessment," *Annals of the American Academy of Political and Social Science*, 322 (March, 1959), 20–29; as reprinted in Stratton and Terry, *Prevention of Delinquency*, p. 317.

43. *Ibid.*, p. 322.

44. John M. Martin, "Three Approaches to Delinquency Prevention: A Critique," *Crime and Delinquency*, 7 (January, 1961), 16–24.

45. See the discussion in Stanton Wheeler, Leonard S. Cottrell, Jr., and Anne Romasco, *Juvenile Delinquency: Its Prevention and Control* (New York: Russell Sage Foundation, 1966), pp. 19–21.

46. President's Commission on Law Enforcement and Administration of Justice, *The Challenge of Crime in a Free Society* (Washington, D.C.: U.S. Government Printing Office, 1967), p. 1.

47. See, for example, Schur, *Our Criminal Society: The Social and Legal Sources of Crime in America* (Englewood Cliffs, N.J.: Prentice-Hall, Inc., 1969).

48. William Ryan, *Blaming the Victim*, Vintage Books (New York: Random House, Inc., 1972), p. 7.

49. Milton L. Barron, *The Juvenile in Delinquent Society* (New York: Alfred A. Knopf, Inc., 1954).

50. Walter D. Connor, *Deviance in Soviet Society: Crime, Delinquency, and Alcoholism* (New York: Columbia University Press, 1972), p. 94.

51. See discussion in Schur, *Our Criminal Society*, pp. 73–81 and 233–34; also for a diversity of views and findings, see Otto N. Larsen, ed., *Violence and the Mass Media* (New York: Harper & Row, Publishers, 1968).

NEW WAYS OF LOOKING AT DELINQUENCY

Much of the disenchantment with current delinquency policy arises from the simple fact that it doesn't work. As we have seen, neither the treatment reaction nor the reform response has provided any real basis for confidence that our measures are effective in preventing delinquent behavior or rehabilitating youthful offenders. Some programs do show more promise than others, but the impact of the specific successes on the overall problem of youthful misbehavior is minimal. A traditional response to this situation has been to assume that the system merely needs improvement. Hence the call for more and better facilities, increasingly experimental rehabilitation schemes, further research—including evaluation studies and elaborate "cost-benefit" and "systems" analyses. Naturally, it is possible by these methods to increase efficiency in juvenile justice and perhaps also to render the substance of the system somewhat more meaningful. Yet the conviction is growing that this kind of patching-up will not suffice. Many observers are coming to believe that our present approaches to delinquency and juvenile justice are *basically* unsound: that the underlying assumptions are all wrong, and that present programs are not just ineffective but positively harmful. This belief arises not only out of direct experience and research in the field of delinquency, but also from current thinking on the broader topic of deviant behavior and social control. Social scientists, and increasingly laymen as well, are reevaluating our society's response to rule-violating behavior. In this chapter, I shall describe some of the major themes of this reevaluation.

LABELING ANALYSIS

One of the most influential strands of current sociological thought in this area is alternatively designated the "labeling," "societal reactions," or "interactionist" approach.[1] According to this perspective, various features of deviance situations are more directly attributable to the impact of social reaction processes than to the personal characteristics or socioeconomic situations of individual offenders. Indeed, the very notion of deviance itself presupposes rules or norms against which the individual has offended. As a leading spokesman for this outlook puts it:

> . . . *social groups create deviance by making the rules whose infraction constitutes deviance*, and by applying these rules to particular people and labeling them as outsiders. From this point of view, deviance is *not* a quality of the act the person commits, but rather a consequence of the application by others of rules and sanctions to an "offender." The deviant is one to whom that label has successfully been applied; deviant behavior is behavior that people so label.[2]

This does not mean that the acts we label burglary, or assault, or car theft would never occur if there were not formal rules defining them. Rather, the argument is that the reactions to such behaviors will largely determine their social meaning and consequences. To that extent, the labeling position is extremely relativistic. Particular acts are not intrinsically "deviant"; their deviant character emerges out of the interaction between offending individuals and the informal and formal responses of reacting individuals and agencies—including official agencies of social control. This crucial definitional aspect of deviance becomes quite clear in the case of some of the more controversial elements in delinquency laws. Thus, if one were to remove from such laws categories like "incorrigibility" or "associating with bad companions," it is unlikely that youthful behavior would change very much. However, the social meanings and consequences of various kinds of behavior might be dramatically altered. "Incorrigibility" is in large measure a judgment that some people pass on other people; it is not an objective behavioral category on the meaning of which we would all agree. Platt referred to this conferral of meaning and elaboration of consequence when he subtitled his book on the juvenile justice movement "The Invention of Delinquency." [3]

A societal reactions perspective, then, is more concerned with what is made of an act socially than with the factors that may have led particular individuals into the behavior in the first place. While these precipitating factors obviously have some importance, the labeling analysts believe they have been overemphasized. Many of the reaction processes that shape deviance situations remain crucial, they argue, *whatever* the precipitating factors in specific cases may be. In particular, the labeling approach stresses that the self-concepts and long-term behavior of rule-violators are vitally influenced by the interaction between them and agents of social control. The application of this notion to delinquency is far from new, a classic illustration being Tannenbaum's discussion of the "dramatization of evil" through which the early stigmatizing of a youngster as a trouble maker helps to propel him into a delinquent career:

> The process of making the criminal, therefore, is a process of tagging, defining, identifying, segregating, describing, emphasizing, making conscious and self-conscious; it becomes a way of stimulating, suggesting, emphasizing, and evoking the very traits that are complained of. . . .

The person becomes the thing he is described as being. Nor does it seem to matter whether the valuation is made by those who would punish or by those who would reform. . . . The harder they work to reform the evil, the greater the evil grows under their hands. The persistent suggestion, with whatever good intentions, works mischief, because it leads to bringing out the bad behavior that it would suppress. The way out is through a refusal to dramatize the evil.[4]

There is, then, a complex process, of response and counter-response beginning with an initial act of rule-violation and developing into elaborated delinquent self-conceptions and a full-fledged delinquent career. The labeling or societal reactions orientation helps us see that "delinquent" (indeed, as I suggested earlier, even "juvenile") is what the sociologist terms an *ascribed status*—it is a social position one occupies not simply as a consequence of one's own action, but also as a result of the actions of others. To understand delinquency, therefore, one studies not only the rule-violators themselves, but also those who react to them.

Deviance is not a property *inherent* in certain forms of behavior; it is a property *conferred upon* these forms by the audiences which directly or indirectly witness them. Sociologically, then, the critical variable is the social *audience* . . . since it is the audience which eventually decides whether or not any given action or actions will become a visible case of deviation.[5]

STEREOTYPING. As I have suggested elsewhere,[6] the interaction through which deviant status or identity is conferred on individuals involves several key processes—stereotyping, retrospective interpretation, and negotiation. Although stereotyping is most often associated with racial prejudice and discrimination, the same process is quite evident in crime and delinquency. We are likely to have specific ideas of what "criminals" and "delinquents" are like, even if we have never had any direct encounters with known law-violators. Reactions based on these stereotypes may significantly affect how individuals are treated throughout the various stages in the administration of juvenile justice. Indeed, the considerable discretion vested in officials at all levels of the juvenile justice system makes them vulnerable to the influence of stereotypical thinking. According to a major study of police encounters with juveniles:

> . . . both the decision made in field—whether or not to bring the boy in—and the decision made at the station—which disposition to invoke—were based largely on cues which emerged from the interaction between the officer and the youth, cues from which the officer inferred the youth's character. These cues included the youth's group affiliations, age, race, grooming, dress, and demeanor. Older juveniles, members of known delinquent gangs, Negroes, youths with well-oiled hair, black jackets, and soiled denims or jeans (the presumed uniform of "tough" boys), and boys who in their interactions with officers did not manifest what were considered to be appropriate signs of respect tended to receive the more severe dispositions.[7]

Similarly, the philosophy of the juvenile court—with its thoroughgoing social investigation of the alleged delinquent, and its relative lack of concern with the particular offense—virtually ensures that stereotypes will influence judicial dispositions. Sending the child who comes from a "broken home" in the slums to a training school, while giving probation to a youngster from a "good family" may not strike the judge as an exercise in stereotyping. He will justify his decisions on the basis of experience, or "theory," and consider them to be in the best interests of all concerned. As we have seen, however, such stereotypes tend to be self-confirming. Children from "broken homes" are likely to be committed to institutions because they are believed to be delinquency-prone; yet these very commitments, in turn, serve to reinforce that belief.

RETROSPECTIVE INTERPRETATION. Retrospective interpretation is the process by which once an individual is identified as deviant, he is seen in a totally "new light." The very category "delinquent" invests an individual with distinguishing personal characteristics, and also a completely new personal identity:

> The work of the denunciation effects the recasting of the objective character of the perceived other: The other person becomes in the eyes of his condemners literally a different and *new* person. It is not that the new attributes are added to the old "nucleus."

> He is not changed, he is reconstituted. . . . The former identity stands as accidental; the new identity is the "basic reality." What he is now is what, "after all," he was all along.[8]

Undoubtedly the most dramatic way of setting this process in motion is through a public "status-degradation ceremony" such as the criminal trial. One day the individual is simply an ordinary citizen, the next (as a result of conviction, or perhaps merely accusation) he has suddenly been converted into a "murderer," a "burglar," or whatever. And from then on he is seen *only* in terms of this new (degraded) status. Because of the attempt to develop less harsh and nonadversary procedures in juvenile cases, youths who come before the juvenile court may experience a somewhat less severe identity-stripping. Yet the individual's character (past as well as present) is reread just as much when he is adjudicated as a delinquent as it would if he were convicted on criminal charges. In fact, concepts like "delinquency proneness," and "predelinquent," are in a sense devices through which retrospective interpretations may be applied. Many of the studies employing these concepts have arrived at them, it will be recalled, retrospectively—by interpreting characteristics found in already-adjudicated delinquents as "indicators" of a supposedly preexistent disposition. Similarly, when the judge considers the results of the probation officer's investigation for "sentencing" purposes, he discovers early indicators of likely wrongdoing that enable him to impose junishment with an easier conscience and with a presumed psychological or sociological rationale.

Recent analyses have revealed the special role of the "case record" or "case history" in recasting the deviant's identity. Goffman has argued that the content of dossiers on mental patients is one-sided. What they are *not* regularly used for is

> . . . to record occasions when the patient showed capacity to cope honorably and effectively with difficult life situations. Nor is the case record typically used to provide a rough average or sampling of his past conduct. One of its purposes is to show the ways in which patient is sick and the reasons why it was right to commit him and is right currently to keep him committed, and

this is done by abstracting from his whole life course a list of those incidents that have or might have had "symptomatic" significance.[9]

Of course, those who make and use the record are not engaged in some underhanded plot, nor are they consciously falsifying the facts. But, as Goffman goes on to stress, "almost anyone's life course could yield up enough denigrating facts to provide grounds for the record's justification of commitment."[10] It is true that in delinquency cases, the life experience from which the recorder can draw relevant clues and incidents is more compressed. On the other hand, given the extreme vagueness with which delinquency and alleged predispositions to delinquency are defined, and the wide range of presumed indicators employed, a retrospective interpretation that such predisposition existed could easily be made for almost any child. I referred earlier to the way in which this process may ease decision-making for those who must pass judgment on alleged delinquents. As one commentator has acutely observed, these processes of "biographical reconstruction" strain toward a consistency that colors most imputations of deviance: "the social need of Others to render Actors as consistent objects. . . . There must be a *special* history that *specially* explains current imputed identity. Relative to deviance, the *present evil* of current character must be related to past evil that can be discovered in biography."[11] We can see at work here both the "evil causes evil" fallacy, and the need to see rule-violators as fundamentally different from nonviolators.

NEGOTIATION. The third component in deviance-imputation processes, negotiation, is again more blatantly evident in cases involving adults than in those involving youthful offenders—the best example being the phenomenon of "plea bargaining" in criminal trials.[12] Sociologists have noted, however, that since the labeling of deviants involves the imposition of some peoples' rules and definitions on others, an element of negotiation or bargaining (however covert or informal) is almost always present. Thus it has been argued that even in psychiatric diagnosis there is a subtle interplay between psychiatrist and patient, out of which emerges a definition of the situation on the basis of which treatment can proceed.[13] If the psychiatric patient, even under conditions of voluntary submission to diagnosis and therapy, is in a relatively weak position from which to bargain about the terms of the doctor-patient relationship, the youth who is compulsorily proceeded against for alleged delinquency is in an even weaker situation. Young people in our society hold relatively little effective social power under any circumstances. Furthermore, the procedures are built around the idea that specialists know better than the individual himself what is "in his best interest."

Nevertheless, the alleged delinquent often does try to influence his disposition; he may be alert to and try to exploit the relationship between the image he presents and the probable outcome of his case. This possibility is nicely depicted in the song from *West Side Story,* in which the youngster assures the police officer that he is "deprived" and not "depraved." Perhaps the major bargaining area concerns imputations of "guilt" versus imputations of "disturbance." As one study of the interaction between juveniles and probation officers disclosed, this subtle bargaining relates closely to the process of retrospective interpretation:

> . . . a juvenile who is "appealing and attractive" and who "wants very much to be liked and relates in a friendly manner to all around her," is a prime candidate for clinical interpretations as opposed to criminal imputations. Finding "problems" in the home is not difficult. . . . The transformation of the juvenile into a sick object permits all concerned to suspend the criminal imputations of her acts, even though the penal code sections are quoted every time the police report theft or burglary.[14]

As labeling theorists emphasize, once an individual has been branded as a wrongdoer, it becomes extremely difficult for him to shed that new identity. Tannenbaum expressed this most aptly when he wrote of the delinquent or criminal that, "the community expects him to live up to his reputation, and will not credit him if he does not live up to it."[15] Both the general process of retrospective interpretation, and the more specific uses of the case history or case record, seem to be centrally involved in creating obstacles to what is sometimes termed "deviance-disavowal." Because the branding of an individual as a "delinquent" or a "criminal" often will imply a broad recasting of identity, the person so stigmatized is hard put to convince others he is not really, or no longer, "like that." And if anyone is unclear as to his real character, there is always the "record" testifying to his basic unworthiness. As we noted earlier, the claim that youths proceeded against in juvenile court do not obtain a "record" is far from convincing. In fact—and regardless of whether or not an official dossier is available to others for scrutiny—the taint from such a proceeding may often surround the individual for many years. Typically, these negative labeling processes snowball. A stigmatizing experience imposes new restrictions on legitimate opportunities and raises the probabilities of further deviation, which in turn will give rise to more serious negative reactions, and so on. And the public tendency to believe that "once a wrongdoer, always a wrongdoer," reinforces these vicious circles.

This does not mean that a single contact with officialdom automatically triggers a life of crime. In fact we know that very many children who have come before juvenile courts do not "graduate" to adult criminality. There are a number of reasons why this is so. The impact of labeling processes on the self-concepts of youngsters may be far from uniform. On the one hand, to the extent that children are more vulnerable and impressionable than adults, the effects of being treated as a bad person could be especially pronounced. On the other hand, given the situational and sporadic nature of much youthful misconduct (a point to which we shall return in the next chapter), it is relatively easy for some youngsters to develop social-psychological mechanisms to insulate themselves from imputations of bad character. As the earlier discussion of bargaining and negotiation should suggest, differentials in power resources may significantly affect these outcomes.

This is where some of the standard sociological variables come into play in labeling analysis, which initially focuses less directly on socioeconomic background than on the individual's interaction with control agents and other "audiences". In our society, lower-class children more than middle-class ones, black children more than white ones, and boys more than girls, face high probabilities (i.e., run a special "categorical risk" in the actuarial sense) not only of engaging in rule-violation in the first place, but also of becoming enmeshed in official negative labeling processes. By the same token, their social positions afford them fewer resources with which to withstand the degrading consequences of such labeling. This notion of categorical differences in vulnerability, however, is only a rough generalization; inevitably there will be individual variation in susceptibility and resistance to labeling within any one of these social categories. The labeling approach, then, does not assert that the stigmatizing process is simple, direct, or unvarying. It has, however, alerted us to the strong possibility that various kinds of intervention in the lives of children may have these effects; indeed that such intervention often may do more harm than good.

More generally, it has redirected deviance analysis away from the largely inconclusive comparison of supposed offenders and nonoffenders toward intensive exploration of the interaction between rule-violators and those who respond to their behavior. The emphasis increasingly has turned toward the processes of control. As Lemert recently commented, traditional sociological approaches "tended to rest heavily upon the idea that deviance leads to social control. I have come to believe that the reverse idea, i.e., social control leads to social deviance, is equally tenable and the potentially richer premise for studying deviance in modern society. . . ." [16] This new attention to reaction processes, and to the official control agents and agencies, is producing an increasingly sophisticated and realistic assessment of deviance problems and policies. Some specific ways in which this assessment illuminates juvenile justice processes and institutions are discussed below.

THE UNMASKING OF EUPHEMISM

At first glance, it might seem as though only the specific labels that are applied to individuals are important. If that were true, then it might also follow that calling a youngster a "delinquent" rather than a "criminal," or "adjudicating" him instead of "convicting" him, would make a big difference. Yet this is far from what the labeling analysts have in mind. On the contrary, their major focus has been on the *quality* of the social reaction and the nature of its impact, not on the wording of the label. Indeed, the labeling approach—as part of a more general willingness to closely scrutinize various social institutions and processes—actually has revealed that much of this euphemistic renaming has little if any bearing on the real social meaning and consequence of what is renamed.

To some extent this growing skepticism arises from the patent ineffectiveness of the optimistically designated processes and programs. Thus, the term "rehabilitation" has lost much of its earlier attractiveness because of the obvious failure to rehabilitate. Likewise, the substantial failure to treat or to train has cast such terminology as "treatment institution" and "training school" into considerable disrepute. It remains to be seen whether currently modish concepts such as "community participation" and "therapeutic milieu" will eventuate in the same disillusionment. But it is not merely the absence of favorable results that has unmasked the euphemisms in this area. A recognition of the probability of distinctly harmful results also has been growing. Here the traditional sociological focus on the objective consequences of institutions and actions—especially the possible unintended consequences—becomes particularly helpful. Such objective consequences, the sociologist stresses, should be considered apart from any conscious purposes or motives. Thus, while many delinquency policies and programs are motivated by the well-intended conviction that they are in the "best interests" of the children involved, their objective effects show the contrary. Many observers would question whether anyone other than the individual himself is really qualified to say what is in his best interests. But apart from that thorny issue, there is now widespread recognition that the legal processing of juveniles, whatever it is called and however it is described, is in fact significantly punitive and potentially stigmatizing. This first became clear in the commitment to institutions, which function as "schools for crime." As a recent report prepared for the American Friends Service Committee stated (referring primarily to adult imprisonment—but most of the comments also apply to juvenile commitments):

> Where "progressive penology" rules, the changes are trivial when measured against the magnitude of penal coercion's human cost. We submit that the basic evils of imprisonment are that it denies

autonomy, degrades dignity, impairs or destroys self-reliance, in-
culcates authoritarian values, minimizes the likelihood of beneficial interaction with one's peers, fractures family ties, destroys
the family's economic stability, and prejudices the prisoner's
future prospects for any improvement in his economic and social
status. It does all these things *whether or not* the buildings are
antiseptic or dirty, the aroma that of fresh bread or stale urine,
the sleeping accommodation a plank or an innerspring mattress,
or the interaction of inmates takes place in cells and corridors
("idleness") or in the structural setting of a particular time and
place ("group therapy").[17]

If this assessment of the futility of actual piecemeal reforms is correct, then clearly the value of euphemistic labels to negate the
reality of imprisonment is even more negligible.

In recent years awareness of this point has been extended to
cover not only institutional "rehabilitation" efforts but the entire
juvenile court system. It first began with the recognition that under
the court's indeterminate commitment procedures, a youth could
be institutionalized for a longer period of time than he would have
been had he been a few years older (and therefore subject to the
adult criminal law, which often specify maximum penalties). This
is hardly in his "best interests." The broader argument that gradu-
ally emerged has been cogently stated by an early legal critic of the
juvenile court:

It is important . . . to recognize that when, in an authoritative
setting, we attempt to do something *for* a child "because of what
he is and needs," we are also doing something *to* him. The
semantics of "socialized justice" are a trap for the unwary. Whatever one's motivations, however elevated one's objectives, if the
measures taken result in the compulsory loss of the child's liberty,
the involuntary separation of a child from his family, or even
the supervision of a child's activities by a probation worker, the
impact on the affected individuals is essentially a punitive one.
Good intentions and a flexible vocabulary do not alter this reality.
. . . We shall escape much confusion here if we are willing to
give candid recognition to the fact that the business of the
juvenile court inevitably consists, to a considerable degree, in
dispensing punishment.[18]

As is well known, this line of argument has been the basis for many of the more specific criticisms of procedural laxity in juvenile justice, such as gave rise to the aforementioned Supreme Court decision in the *Gault* case. But this insistence on facing up to the punitive reality of ostensibly beneficent legal control over the individual has occurred on a number of fronts at once, not only in criminal and juvenile justice. For example, compulsory treatment of drug addicts and persons diagnosed as mentally ill has similarly been challenged partly on the grounds that such treatment constitutes punishment, euphemistic designations and paternalistic statements of good intent notwithstanding.[19] All of these challenges also reflect the recent rethinking by legal scholars of the proper role and scope of the criminal law as a general mechanism of social control.

A final point that should be made about euphemism is the possible harm produced by its very use—quite apart from its function in diverting attention away from harsh realities. It may well be, for example, that all the talk in juvenile court about "rehabilitation" and "personalized justice" leads to considerable confusion or even mocking contempt on the part of the youths being proceeded against. Asserting that various features of their court processing cause juveniles to develop a definite "sense of injustice," David Matza considers how a youth might view the behavior of the officials he encounters there:

> . . . the suspicion that he is being misled regarding the basis of disposition suggests the necessity of exploratory speculation regarding the true bases. Why should persons so important and influential as the judge and his helpers lie to him regarding the true bases of disposition? Why should they insist, as they frequently do, that it is not what he did—which strikes delinquents and others as a sensible reason for legal intervention—but his underlying problems and difficulties that guide court action? Why do they say they are helping him when patently they are limiting his freedom of action and movement by putting him on probation or in prison? What on earth could they possibly be hiding that would lead them to such heights of deception?[20]

If, as I shall suggest later, the question of youthful misbehavior is in a sense as much a political issue as a scientific one, then the reactions of those processed by the juvenile court become especially important. For if American youth confronts legal institutions it cannot respect, calls for obedience and "law and order" may be to little avail.

THE ORGANIZATIONAL FACTOR

Another body of work that has significantly broadened our perspectives on juvenile justice is organizational analysis. We have already seen some of the ways in which this kind of analysis can increase our understanding of residential treatment institutions. Confusion over organizational goals, problems of informal inmate social systems, intrastaff conflicts, and the difficulties of maintaining smooth relations with a variety of external forces, all greatly influence the workings of these institutions. These and other key organizational features have been illuminated by research that only sometimes has arisen out of an interest in delinquency problems; more often, the researchers' prime concern has been to explore the structure and dynamics of organizations in general—implications for the study of delinquency frequently have been unintended byproducts of such inquiries.

The organization's impact on individual clients is most clearly evident in treatment institutions, particularly those units that display features of what Goffman has called the "total institution"—in which harsh identity-stripping and mortification processes and all-enveloping organizational routine resocialize the individual to his new inmate role.[21] But researchers are beginning to demonstrate that other units involved in the processing of delinquents—such as police departments, probation offices, psychiatric clinics, and the juvenile court itself—also relate to their "clients" *as organizations,* and illustrate many of the concepts and theories of organizational or institutional analysis. From an organizational standpoint the problem of delinquency is to some extent one of *management:* "What may be and usually is a crisis and an emergency to the person experiencing this official processing is, from the point of view of the official and the agency for which he works, simply a matter of organizational routine." Thus, one sees the bureaucratization of deviance: "deviants come under the regulation of hierarchy, impersonality, specialization, and systematic formal rules." [22] Indeed, the administration of juvenile justice may be viewed as a delinquency-processing "system"—the coordination, organizational specificity, and rule-consistency of which vary considerably from time to time and place to place. Individuals are passed from one stage (or one unit) to another—along what Rubington and Weinberg nicely term a "deviance corridor"—with selection processes occurring and cases "dropping out" at each stage.

ORGANIZATIONAL NEEDS

What this bureaucratization most significantly implies is that the *needs of the organization* often affect and even determine the nature of delinquency-processing. This factor frequently has a greater bearing on the outcomes in delinquency cases than either the supposed needs of the processed individuals or the specific details of their law-violating behavior. Organizational needs partly center around the sheer necessity of getting a job done, of managing an overwhelming number of cases. As we saw earlier, this problem is glaringly present in probation work, where the ratio of probation officers to probationers vitally affects the nature and quality of supervision. Indeed, these pressures probably influence the operations and dispositions of almost all delinquency-processing units.

The desire to maintain or develop a particular organizational style also determines the outcomes in delinquency processing. One comparative study of police departments found that "professionalization" (as seen in the high degree of centralization and coordination, formal, impersonal rules, careful record-keeping, and the application of "universalistic" standards) results in greater severity (if also greater even-handedness) in the disposition of possible delinquency cases. Although officers in a professionalized department held somewhat more sophisticated ideas about delinquency than those in a less centralized and informal "fraternal" one, they produced a considerably higher juvenile arrest rate.[23] What happens to a kid on the street, then, may be not simply a result of what he has done or which particular police officer he encounters, but of general features of organizational structure and work style.

Aspects of the juvenile court system itself are revealed more and more through organizational or institutional analysis, which now supplements the early legal critiques. Research has indicated that the multiplicity of goals, complex relations with other agencies and the local community, and intrastaff conflict are major factors influencing the court's work. As a consultant to the President's Crime Commission noted, "The court is expected simultaneously to preserve the institution of law, to enhance the legitimate interest of its clients, especially those of children, and to serve the welfare of the community while protecting public order." And in all of this, he went on to emphasize, there are numerous other state and local organizations with which the juvenile court "must maintain complex and multi-level relations in order to achieve stability and effectiveness." [24]

Some of these complex functions and relationships are spelled out in the recent study of a specific juvenile court located in a large northern metropolitan area.[25] There, it was found that the general tenor and detailed procedures of the court's operation were heavily influenced by the judges, and especially by the chief judge who served as head administrator with the power to hire, decide policy, and supervise. Policies reflecting the judges' outlooks, however, were mediated through a complex network of internal staff relations (primarily with probation officers, but also involving defense lawyers and court-associated clinicians), relations with outside agencies (police, school system, welfare agencies), and other forces in the local community. The probation officer, in this system, occupied a pivotal, but quite ambiguous position:

> On the one hand, he performs the routine chores which keep the court operation going. His court work provides his occupational identification and elicits a great deal of commitment on his part. On the other hand, the probation officer has low professional

status within the court itself, relative to both judges and clinic personnel. Furthermore, he is the organizational subordinate of the judges; probation officers hold their jobs at least partially at the discretion of the chief judge. . . . However, the probation officer's practical knowledge and experience tend to offset this low professional and hierarchical standing.[26]

In tracing out the external relationships of the court, Emerson found that the court's dispositions were influenced considerably by outside factors. Judges were political appointees who had no prior experience in delinquency or child welfare work. Examining a number of specific incidents and controversies surrounding the court's work, Emerson concluded that, "politically important segments of the local community, rather than the city's social agencies and social welfare professionals, provide the juvenile court's primary 'constituency.' "[27] The court's relations with the police were also complex. Because so much of the police work with juveniles consisted of informal handling of relatively minor or ambiguous complaints, when the police did bring a case before the juvenile court, Emerson found, it was usually an especially troublesome one for which they sought stern court action. In maintaining smooth working relations with the police, the court had to honor the demand of the police to serve as a "back-up institution," while at the same time try to avoid stigmatizing youths as much as possible. Because of its relation to other processing agencies, the court can control labeling processes as well as contribute to them. With this in mind, it can be argued that "the goal of minimizing court stigmatization requires not only limiting court jurisdiction . . . but also maximizing its power and inclination to resist and change established definitions and proscriptions about delinquents and their situations."[28]

An understanding of the overall delinquency-processing system therefore requires close attention to these organizational elements and difficulties. Typically, this "system" is uncoordinated, inconsistent, and confused. For example, researchers who established the Midcity Youth Project found the existing organizational network beset by "multiplicity, ambiguity of jurisdiction, and lack of consensus as to causes and cures." More specifically, "Police, courts, schools, civil associations, parents' groups, churches, social welfare agencies, mental health organizations, and other groups were engaged on various levels and in various ways in diffuse and uncoordinated attempts to cope with a problem whose parameters they could but dimly perceive and whose remedy was obscure and elusive." [29] Similar conditions prevail even within the narrower complex of official agencies that process delinquents. This is hardly surprising, since juvenile court judges, policemen, probation officers, and psychiatrists come from a variety of socioeconomic backgrounds, have had divergent kinds of professional training, and display strongly varying outlooks on delinquency. When these variations are combined with the differences in needs, interests, goals, and modes of operation of the agencies themselves, the enormous potential for conflict and confusion becomes obvious. Nor is there any coordinating mechanism to reduce the confusion:

> . . . in the field of delinquency control, there is no clear authority channel for the resolution of disagreements. Police systems operate largely on the local and municipal level, probation and the courts operate on a district or county level, and correctional facilities operate on the state level. When psychiatric services are made available, they are typically organized through state mental health units, although their actual services may occur at the level of the district court. The point is simply that there is no single centralized agency that operates throughout the process. Providing that each group remains within legal bounds, none has the right to tell the other how to do their work.[30]

Another typical organizational factor is *vested interests*. Organizations, quite understandably, have an overriding interest in their own survival, and consequently oppose strongly any policies that directly threaten their continued existence. Aside from that major threat, however, they react to proposed changes partly in terms of how such changes affect their established interests. Debates about delinquency policy, therefore, do not necessarily concern only the relative substantive merits of alternative programs. Spokesmen for particular approaches, at least those actively engaged in the programs being considered, have a more than theoretical stake in the outcome. This is the kind of thing a skeptical social observer might look for in almost any situation, but in a field such as that of delinquency policy—involving, as it does, both the "helping" professions and "impartial" legal officials—there may be a certain resistance to acknowledging its existence.[31]

Although many aspects of organizational analysis that are applied to delinquency processing stem from research and theorizing that have no direct relation to the labeling analysis, by and large the focus complements the emphases of the labeling approach. Formal control agents and agencies are among the most direct of the negative labelers, and as such are a natural object for labeling research. And from a societal reactions viewpoint it can be said that, in a sense, organizations produce deviants—in this case delinquents. It has even been suggested that official delinquency statistics, long derided by sociologists as misrepresentative and misleading, may warrant new consideration. While these statistics do not provide a meaningful picture of the characteristics of delinquents, they do more directly indicate the "output" of the processing organizations.[32] Since organizations (as well as delinquents) "produce" delinquency rates, their practices have to be viewed as a key variable in any broad explanation of delinquency problems.

NEO-ANTIDETERMINISM

There has also been an increased willingness to question the deterministic assumptions underlying most traditional causation theories. As we have already seen, most causal explanations—those of both the treatment and reform perspectives—have centered around some notion of constraint. Forces beyond the individual's control are thought to be pushing him into delinquent behavior. In his discussion of traditional delinquency theories, Matza is highly critical of this reliance on conceptions of constraint. Noting that these theories rarely consider the phenomenon of "maturing out" (i.e., that most delinquents do not go on to become adult offenders), he also asserts that "they predict too much delinquency even during the period of optimum involvement." After all, the designa-

tion "delinquent" is relative; one does not spend all one's time vio-
lating the law. As Matza properly insists, "Delinquency is a status
and delinquents are incumbents who *intermittently* act out a
role. . . . The novice practitioner or researcher is frequently amazed
at 'how like other kids' the delinquent can be when he is so in-
clined." [33] As an alternative to the deterministic and oppositional
themes developed in theories of the delinquent subculture, Matza
proposes a concept of drift, which he feels avoids "hard determinism" without positing complete freedom of will or action:

> The image of the delinquent I wish to convey is one of drift; an
> actor neither compelled nor committed to deeds nor freely
> choosing them; neither different in any simple or fundamental
> sense from the law abiding, nor the same; conforming to certain
> traditions in American life while partially unreceptive to other
> more conventional traditions; and finally, an actor whose moti-
> vational system may be explored along lines explicitly com-
> mended by classical criminology—his peculiar relation to legal
> institutions. . . .
>
> Drift stands midway between freedom and control. Its basis is
> an area of the social structure in which control has been loosened,
> coupled with the abortiveness of adolescent endeavor to organize
> an autonomous subculture, and thus an independent source of
> control, around illegal action. The delinquent *transiently* exists
> in a limbo between convention and crime, responding in turn to
> the demands of each, flirting now with one, now the other, but
> postponing commitment, evading decision. Thus, he drifts be-
> tween criminal and conventional action. [34]

This formulation has been extremely influential in reorienting
sociological attempts to explain delinquency. As we shall see in the
next chapter, there now is a substantial body of sociological analysis
that conceives of delinquency in these fluid, contingent, and situational terms. It should be apparent, too, that this approach to
delinquent behavior accords well with premises of the labeling
perspective, in which contingencies of societal reaction contribute
heavily to delinquent outcomes. Both lines of analysis rest on an
interactionist view which asserts that human behavior emerges out
of continuous processes of social interaction. Social situations, under

this view, reflect "an emergent quality that may not have existed before the parties came together." [35] This dynamic emphasis implies both a special conception of the nature of delinquent acts and a distinctive methodology for delinquency research. In fact, the two are very closely intertwined. The research strategies of the static conception of delinquency are no longer acceptable, for such statistical comparisons and cross-tabulations impose an artificial clarity and rigidity on what are in fact extremely fluid processes.

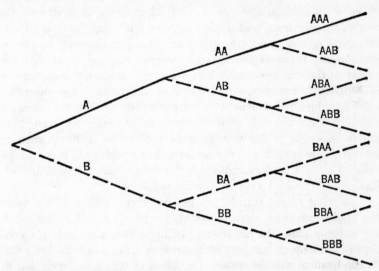

In his general discussion of deviance theories, Cohen has nicely suggested that the interactionist view is better depicted by a "tree" diagram than in the traditional multicelled table. He comments:

> . . . the deviant act develops over time through a series of stages. Some individual, in the pursuit of some interest or goal, and taking account of the situation, makes a move, possibly in a deviant direction, possibly with no thought of deviance in mind. However, his next move—the continuation of his course of action—is not fully determined by the state of affairs at the beginning. He may, at this juncture, choose among two or more possible directions. Which it will be will depend on the state of the actor and situation at *this* point in time, and either or both may,

in the meantime, have undergone change. . . . The completed pathway A, AA, AAA—here represented by solid line—is the course of action that, according to the theory, culminates in deviance. The other pathways, represented by broken lines, are the other courses that action *could* have taken. Pathways are not predictable from initial states or initial acts alone; prediction is *contingent* on the state of affairs following each move.[36]

This statement indicates very clearly how the new dynamic perspective on delinquency (as well as other forms of deviance) diverges sharply from traditional outlooks, with their notions of differentiation, constraint, and predictability. Furthermore, the interrelationship between theory and research method is nicely conveyed in these comments. We can see why statistical comparisons of supposedly matched samples cannot adequately show the processes by which delinquent acts, self-concepts, and "careers" emerge; although they are still used in much delinquency research, they are increasingly giving way to more qualitative methods such as intensive observation and the use of autobiographies in order to develop a deeper understanding of the interaction between the offender and those who respond to his behavior.

To what extent sociologists generally are willing to set aside the well-entrenched ideas of social determinism and constraint is not entirely clear. In his recent writings, Matza extends his concept of drift by elaborating on the role of *will* in deviant behavior. At the heart of this discussion is a notion of option—nobody *has* to become a deviant (in the sense of a rigid individual determinism), but virtually anyone might (should the proper conjuncture of inclination and situation present itself). Both the inception of deviant activity and its continuation depend, in Matza's formulation, on the individual himself.

By being willing, the subject may begin a process that neither holds him within its grip nor unfolds without him. . . . To enter the process, the invitational edge of the deviant phenomenon must somehow be hurdled. To do that a leap is required—an act of will; the phenomenon is engaged, but not abstractly. The subject is actually doing the thing—an immersion in concrete

reality which is essential. The remainder of the process of becoming deviant can hardly happen if the subject continues to
gaze at a phenomenon kept at a distance.[37]

Most sociologists probably would resist pushing this concept of
will too far, and would continue to place equal or greater significance on the fact that individuals, by virtue of their positions in
the socioeconomic order, differ greatly in the freedom with which
they can actively shape their behavior. At the same time, Matza's
formulation has been very important in nurturing an appreciation
of the fluidity and openness of action situations, and has helped
enable researchers to recognize the significant role of labeling and
other contingencies. Likewise, although the public policy implications of this new look at determinism are not entirely clear, it certainly has heightened disenchantment with those paternalistic policies that conventional theories have fostered and reinforced.

DEVIANCE AND POLITICS

Crime and delinquency are inherently political phenomena.
This is so for at least two reasons: because public policy decisions
of various sorts shape the social structures and value systems within
which such behavior occurs; and because ultimately the substance
of crime and delinquency laws is, as we have seen, a matter for
political decision.[38] Furthermore, as one perceptive analyst has
stressed, "the interests represented in the formulation and administration of public policy are those treasured by the dominant segments of the society. Hence, public policy is created because segments with power differentials are in conflict with one another.
Public policy itself is a manifestation of an interest structure in
politically organized society." [39] Similarly, another influential study
recently asserted that "deviance is the name of the conflict game
in which individuals or loosely organized small groups with little
power are strongly feared by a well-organized, stable minority or
majority who have a large amount of power." [40]

Conventional deviance theories, including those on delinquency, have often obscured this central power element, which was overshadowed by all the attention paid to the supposedly distinguishing characteristics of offenders and to subcultural factors. Now, particularly under the influence of the labeling approach—with its direct focus on rule-making and rule-applying—this selective inattention to conflict and power is being righted. The very process of designating an individual as "delinquent" is coming to be recognized as an imposition of social power, as a political act in the broadest sense of the term.

During this period of rapid social change, it becomes increasingly difficult to draw a sharp distinction between individual deviance and social or political conflict. Political and social movements violate laws to further their goals, while persons we earlier would have labeled individual deviants (drug addicts, homosexuals, ex-prisoners) are organizing and engaging in political action in support of their collective interests. With this heightened political consciousness, few remain unaware of the political implications of deviance policies: "As the politicization of deviance develops, the hidden conflict will become visible and deviants can be expected to demand changes in the configuration of the social hierarchy." [41] There is a continuing struggle between those who seek to define an issue raised by socially problematic behavior as political (reflecting a clash between social movements) and those who attempt to label it individual deviance.

Conflicting interpretations of contemporary American "youth culture" illustrate this point. There are those who would deny the very notion of a youth culture, who consider any reference to "the movement" as an unwarranted attempt to politicize diverse patterns of individual deviance. These observers would probably view as particularly inappropriate any attempt to interpret delinquency in political terms.[42] However, according to an increasingly influential line of analysis, delinquency as well as other forms of youthful rule-violation should indeed be viewed as partially political because it reflects general alienation from an unacceptable socioeconomic structure and cultural value system, and constitutes a forerunner of major sociocultural change. Much of the groundwork for this interpretation was laid down by Paul Goodman in his early social critique *Growing Up Absurd,* a major theme of which was that "the accumulation of the missed and compromised revolutions of modern times, with their consequent ambiguities and social imbalances, has fallen, and must fall, most heavily on the young, making it hard to grow up." [43]

More recent discussions of a youthful "counterculture" similarly have emphasized an alienation from, and questioning of, the basic premises of a technocratic and materialistic society. [44] According to a perceptive sociological student of these matters, this youth culture now has an exceedingly broad membership base and an increasingly political orientation:

> . . . a general "youth culture" that attracts the interest and participation of young people of many social strata and geographic regions has emerged for the first time in our history. Previously, the culture that separated the adolescent and youth population from adult roles was segmented into a variety of discrete subcultures and styles. During the past decade, young people of many types have increasingly come to share an overarching common set of symbols and attitudes. To be sure, distinct differences distinguish the white middle-class youth culture from black ghetto youth culture, but even these cultures share some common symbols and sometimes seek alliances with each other.
>
> Moreover, the new national youth culture, unlike the "teenage" expressions of the thirties, forties, and fifties, contains strong elements of explicit opposition to the prevailing adult culture. Significantly, many of its active spokesmen see the youth culture not as a transitional experience, but as a *counter* culture—that is, a definite challenge to the values and norms that are officially proclaimed and institutionalized in the larger society.
>
> Second, during the past decade, youth has engaged in oppositional radical and revolutionary politics on a scale never before experienced in this country. Moreover, it has done so as youth, with little or no adult control or guidance, and with a strong component of antipathy to adult politics of any variety. [45]

What we are now seeing, according to Flacks, is "a subculture of youth that looked at first like a deviant group but turned out to be a vanguard." [46]

Unquestionably, it would be misleading to picture all delinquents as political rebels, and all delinquency as a social movement. At the same time, this kind of analysis has enormous value in pointing out some central elements in the labeling of delinquency. The disposition to consider youthful behavior (almost by definition) as problematic reflects major power differentials in our society—just as did the tendency to think entirely in terms of a "Negro problem" rather than a problem of institutionalized white racism. At the very least, the counterculture interpretation reminds us that both the making and administering of specific delinquency rules involve an important power aspect.

From this perspective, the reallocation of power may be a prerequisite for successful delinquency policies, at both the local and national levels. Thus, in their comparative analysis of two adjacent Bronx communities in New York City, Martin and his colleagues emphasize, as a key feature of the high-delinquency area, "the lack of any one organization or interest group which could effectively speak for the people of the area and mediate and interpret their needs to the broader community." [47] Commenting more generally on the extent to which the processing of delinquents involves an "ethnocentric exercise of power," these same authors note that alleged principles of mental hygiene (central to the casework-oriented juvenile court system) are being used to rationalize what is actually an unquestioning imposition of middle-class norms. Yet, they insist, "It really has nothing to do with mental hygiene, good or bad. It is a problem of a conflict of values and the issue is the extent to which the community at large is willing to admit the legitimacy of norms and values peculiar to one subgroup or subculture in its midst. When these conflicts of value are made explicit, political processes exist by which they can be accommodated or resolved, sometimes, as noted, by legal coercion." [48] Similarly, the authors of *Struggle for Justice* assert: "Paternalistic trickle-down methods are neither practical nor acceptable. The fundamental reallocations of power and resources that are required can only occur through rapid development by the oppressed and intimidated of their political power so that they can promote and defend their own interests. This in turn requires pride, hope, and organization. But it is those from whom this response is most needed—the blacks, the poor, and the young—who are disproportionately victimized by law enforcement." [49]

LIMITING THE CRIMINAL LAW

There has been a reactivated debate among legal scholars and others on the appropriate and effective uses of the criminal law. This is, of course, a matter that has long preoccupied philosophers and specialists in jurisprudence, but the recently heightened concern with this issue probably dates from the so-called Wolfenden Report, issued in 1957.[50] A British governmental committee was charged to examine the laws relating to homosexual behavior and prostitution, and supported its specific recommendations (the best known of which was the removal of penalties for private homosexual acts between consenting adults) with a major statement on the general functions and limits of the criminal law as a mechanism of social control. The Committee took the position that the criminal law should not intrude into the private lives of citizens, except where necessary to preserve public order and decency, to protect individuals from offensive and injurious behavior, and to guard against exploitation and corruption—particularly of those who might have some special vulnerability. "Unless a deliberate attempt is to be made by society, acting through the agency of the law, to equate the sphere of crime with that of sin, there must remain a realm of private morality and immorality which is, in brief and crude terms, not the law's business. To say this is not to condone or encourage private immorality." [51]

This argument ignited a substantial debate among contemporary legal philosophers, ranging from the critical assertion by Lord Patrick Devlin that "the criminal law as we know it is based upon moral principle. In a number of crimes its function is simply to enforce a moral principle and nothing else," [52] to the tightly reasoned philosophic defense by H. L. A. Hart who insisted, following John Stuart Mill, that we should carefully limit the law's interference with individual liberty.[53] Perhaps the most interesting issue joined in this debate has to do with where the burden of argument and proof should lie in imposing criminal sanctions. While the Committee, and its supporters like Hart, argued that recourse to the criminal law always requires compelling justification, critics like Devlin asserted that the burden of argument lies on those who would overturn long-standing regulations. In the continuing consideration of this issue since the specific debate about the Wolfenden Report, it appears that on balance the former argument has been winning out.

This is so not simply because of its possible philosophic merits, but also because of a great deal of evidence showing the ineffectiveness (and actual harmfulness) of overextending the criminal law. Hart, in the study already cited, and other legal scholars as well,[54] have to some extent explored this aspect of the problem. Such evidence is especially plentiful in "crimes without victims." [55] Here, criminal law tries to control the consensual exchange of widely desired goods or services; major examples are drug use, abortion, various sexual "offenses," and gambling. In part these purported crimes can be said to be victimless because the direct harm, if any, is experienced by the "offenders" themselves—although there can be endless debate regarding the existence of victims in such situations (e.g., the argument that the fetus is a victim in the case of abortion). However they are also victimless in a much more significant sense; because consensual transactions are involved, none of the direct participants is likely to become a complainant to the law-enforcement authorities. The absence of a complaining victim and the consequent difficulty in obtaining evidence hampers enforcement activity tremendously and forces police to rely on highly questionable techniques such as the use of informers, decoys, and electronic surveillance. Even with these methods, given the consensual and usually private nature of the transactions, and the supply-demand factor that frequently raises the economic incentive for illicit "suppliers" (i.e., drug importers and distributors, illegal abortionists), there is virtually no possibility of effective enforcement. And not only are these laws blatantly unworkable, but they set the stage for much secondary crime (theft by addicts to support their habits) and drive many potentially law-abiding citizens into criminal roles and increasingly antisocial outlooks.

While delinquency does not exhibit all the features of the victimless crime situation—for example, the consensual transaction element is not typically present—nonetheless there are some significant similarities. Given the wide range of nebulously defined behaviors covered by the juvenile court laws, much delinquency involves no direct harm committed by one person against another. In many instances, therefore, particularly where provisions (such as "incorrigibility" and "person in need of supervision") not included in the ordinary adult criminal law are invoked, there need be no directly victimized complainant. More typically, a party not directly harmed by any specific acts steps forward "in the interest of," or "on behalf of," the youth in question. Furthermore, another feature of victimless crimes, the glaring lack of any real public consensus on legal proscription, is also present in many delinquency charges. Although the question of consensus usually has been approached only in terms of adult "public opinion," delinquency determinations largely involve the imposition by one segment of the public (adults, and perhaps only a limited proportion of the adult population) of *their* rules on another, less powerful segment of the population—young people.

Our present juvenile justice mechanisms reflect in large measure what law professor Herbert Packer—in an analysis concerned mainly with the adult criminal law, but also relevant to our purposes—has termed a "crime control" model of the criminal process.[56] In contrast to a "due process" model that stresses legal safeguards and reflects a strong suspicion that error is particularly likely to occur under informal nonadjudicative procedures, the crime control model stresses speed and finality. "It follows that extrajudicial processes should be preferred to judicial processes, informal operations to formal ones. . . . Routine, stereotyped procedures are essential if large numbers are being handled. The model that will operate successfully on these presuppositions must be an administrative, almost a managerial, model." [57] Although according to its philosophy, the juvenile court attempts to individualize rather than routinize justice, its emphasis on informal administrative process and its recourse to stereotypes in its actual operations (even as it claims to be treating each case on its own merits) are very much in line with the "crime control" approach. Similarly, when Packer states that "The presumption of guilt is what makes it possible for the system to deal efficiently with large numbers. . . . The supposition is that the screening processes operated by police and prosecutors are reliable indicators of probable guilt," [58] he touches on a feature that underlies the actual workings of the traditional juvenile court. It has generally been assumed that youths coming before the court require some action; indeed, guilt with respect to a specific criminal act is not even considered an important question for the court.

These kinds of analysis, then, are making it more and more difficult to justify the present scope of delinquency legislation. In the recent report, *Struggle for Justice,* it is argued that the criminal law should be considered a last resort in attempting to solve social problems. In determining what behaviors should be prohibited, "values of autonomy, individual dissent, property, and cultural diversity must be weighed, as must the value of reducing human suffering caused by punishing persons for law violations. All these are weighed against the urgency of the need for a high level of compliance with a particular social norm and the possibility of achieving this by law." [59] Because so many critical human values may be threatened by the imposition of criminal sanctions, their use can only be justified when the following conditions obtain:

There is compelling social need to require compliance with a particular norm.

The law and its administration can be applied equally, so that all are weighed with the same scales and so that the human costs of enforcement are spread among the largest feasible number of offenders.

There is no less costly method of obtaining compliance.

There is some substantial basis for assuming that the imposition of punishment will produce greater benefit for society than simply doing nothing.[60]

As should be apparent, under these criteria much of our present delinquency policy is, at the very best, highly questionable.

☦ ☦ ☦

1. In this section I draw on ideas developed in my larger analysis of the labeling perspective. See Edwin M. Schur, *Labeling Deviant Behavior: Its Sociological Significance* (New York: Harper & Row, Publishers, 1971); for a collection of representative studies, see Earl Rubington and Martin Weinberg, eds., *Deviance: The Interactionist Perspective* (New York: The Macmillan Company, 1968).

2. Howard S. Becker, *Outsiders* (New York: Free Press, 1963), p. 9.

3. Anthony M. Platt, *The Child Savers* (Chicago: University of Chicago Press, 1969).

4. Frank Tannenbaum, *Crime and the Community* (Boston: Ginn & Company, 1938), pp. 19–20.

5. Kai T. Erikson, "Notes on the Sociology of Deviance," *Social Problems,* 9 (Spring, 1962), 308.

6. Schur, *Labeling Deviant Behavior.*

7. Irving Piliavin and Scott Briar, "Police Encounters with Juveniles," *American Journal of Sociology,* 69 (September, 1964), 210. For a somewhat contrasting view see Donald J. Black and Albert J. Reiss, Jr., "Police Control of Juveniles," *American Sociological Review,* 35 (February, 1970), 63–77.

8. Harold Garfinkel, "Conditions of Successful Degradation Ceremonies," *American Journal of Sociology,* 61 (March, 1956), 421–22.

9. Erving Goffman, *Asylums,* Anchor Books (New York: Doubleday & Company, Inc., 1961), pp. 155–56.

10. *Ibid.,* p. 159.

11. John Lofland, *Deviance and Identity* (Englewood Cliffs, N.J.: Prentice-Hall, Inc., 1966), p. 150.

12. Donald J. Newman, "Pleading Guilty for Considerations: A Study of Bargain Justice," *Journal of Criminal Law, Criminology, and Police Science,* 46 (March–April, 1956), 780–90; see also Jerome Skolnick, *Justice Without Trial* (New York: John Wiley & Sons, Inc., 1966).

13. Thomas J. Scheff, "Negotiating Reality: Notes on Power in the

Assessment of Responsibility," *Social Problems*, 16 (Summer, 1968), 3–17.

14. Aaron V. Cicourel, *The Social Organization of Juvenile Justice* (New York: John Wiley & Sons, Inc., 1968), p. 132.

15. Tannenbaum, *Crime and the Community*, p. 477.

16. Edwin M. Lemert, *Human Deviance, Social Problems, and Social Control* (Englewood Cliffs, N.J.: Prentice-Hall, Inc., 1967), p. v.

17. American Friends Service Committee, *Struggle for Justice: A Report on Crime and Punishment in America* (New York: Hill and Wang, 1971), p. 33.

18. Francis A. Allen, *The Borderland of Criminal Justice* (Chicago: University of Chicago Press, 1964), p. 18.

19. See for example Thomas Szasz, *Ideology and Insanity* (New York: Doubleday & Company, Inc., 1970).

20. David Matza, *Delinquency and Drift* (New York: John Wiley & Sons, Inc., 1964), pp. 133–34.

21. Goffman, *Asylums*.

22. Rubington and Weinberg, *Deviance*, p. 111.

23. James Q. Wilson, "The Police and the Delinquent in Two Cities," in Wheeler, ed., *Controlling Delinquents* (New York: John Wiley & Sons, Inc., 1968), pp. 9–30.

24. Robert D. Vinter, "The Juvenile Court as an Institution," in President's Commission on Law Enforcement and Administration of Justice, *Task Force Report: Juvenile Delinquency and Youth Crime*, p. 85.

25. Robert M. Emerson, *Judging Delinquents* (Chicago: Aldine, 1969).

26. *Ibid.*, pp. 16–17.

27. *Ibid.*, p. 35.

28. *Ibid.*, p. 275.

29. Walter B. Miller, Rainer C. Baum, and Rosetta McNeil, "Delinquency Prevention and Organizational Relations," in Wheeler, ed., *Controlling Delinquents*, p. 63.

30. Stanton Wheeler, Edna Bonacich, M. Richard Cramer, and Irving K. Zola, "Agents of Delinquency Control: A Comparative Analysis," *ibid.*, p. 33.

31. See, for example, Edwin M. Lemert, *Social Action and Legal Change: Revolution Within the Juvenile Court* (Chicago: Aldine, 1970), especially Ch. 5.

32. John I. Kitsuse and Aaron V. Cicourel, "A Note on the Use of Official Statistics," *Social Problems*, 11 (Fall, 1963), 131–39.

33. Matza, *Delinquency and Drift*, p. 26.

34. *Ibid.*, p. 28.

35. Norman K. Denzin, "Symbolic Interactionism and Ethnomethodology: A Proposed Synthesis," *American Sociological Review*, 34 (December, 1969), 924; see also Herbert Blumer, *Symbolic Interactionism* (Englewood Cliffs, N.J.: Prentice-Hall, Inc., 1969); and Edwin M. Schur, "Reactions to Deviance: A Critical Assessment," *American Journal of Sociology*, 75 (November, 1969), 309–322.

36. Cohen, *Deviance and Control* (Englewood Cliffs, N.J.: Prentice-Hall, Inc., 1966), pp. 43, 44–45.

37. Matza, *Becoming Deviant* (Englewood Cliffs, N.J.: Prentice-Hall, 1969), p. 117.

38. See Schur, *Our Criminal Society*, pp. 1–22.

39. Richard Quinney, *The Social Reality of Crime* (Boston: Little, Brown and Company, 1970), p. 39.

40. Lofland, *Deviance and Identity*, p. 14.

41. Irving Louis Horowitz and Martin Liebowitz, "Social Deviance and Political Marginality: Toward a Redefinition of the Relation Between Sociology and Politics," *Social Problems*, 15 (Winter, 1968), p. 282.

42. For a discussion of diverse views on these matters, see Jack D. Douglas, *Youth in Turmoil*, Center for Studies of Crime and Delinquency, National Institute of Mental Health (Washington, D.C.: U.S. Government Printing Office, 1970).

43. Paul Goodman, *Growing Up Absurd: Problems of Youth in the Organized Society*, Vintage Books (New York: Random House, Inc., 1962), p. 217.

44. Theodore Roszak, *The Making of a Counter Culture: Reflections on the Technocratic Society and Its Youthful Opposition*, Anchor Books (New York: Doubleday & Company, Inc., 1969); Charles A. Reich, *The Greening of America* (New York: Random House, Inc., 1970).

45. Richard Flacks, *Youth and Social Change* (Chicago: Markham Publishing Co., 1971), pp. 17–18.

46. *Ibid.*, p. 51; see also Kenneth Keniston, *Youth and Dissent: The Rise of a New Opposition*, Harvest Books (New York: Harcourt Brace Jovanovich, 1971).

47. Martin, Fitzpatrick, and Gould, *The Analysis of Delinquent Behavior* (New York: Random House, Inc., 1970), p. 156.

48. *Ibid.*, p. 181.

49. *Struggle for Justice*, p. 9.

50. Committee on Homosexual Offences and Prostitution, *Report*,

Home Office, Cmnd. 247 (London: Her Majesty's Stationery Office, 1957).

51. *Ibid.*, p. 24.

52. Patrick Devlin, *The Enforcement of Morals* (London: Oxford University Press, 1965), p. 7.

53. H. L. A. Hart, *Law, Liberty, and Morality* (Stanford, Cal.: Stanford University Press, 1963).

54. See, for example, Allen, *Borderland of Criminal Justice*; Sanford Kadish, "The Crisis of Overcriminalization," *Annals of the American Academy of Political and Social Science*, 347 (November, 1967); and Herbert L. Packer, *The Limits of the Criminal Sanction* (Stanford, Cal.: Stanford University Press, 1968).

55. Edwin M. Schur, *Crimes Without Victims* (Englewood Cliffs, N.J.: Prentice-Hall, Inc., 1965).

56. Packer, *Criminal Sanction*, especially Ch. 8, "Two Models of the Criminal Process."

57. *Ibid.*, p. 159.

58. *Ibid.*, p. 160.

59. *Struggle for Justice*, p. 149.

60. *Ibid.*, p. 66.

RADICAL NONINTERVENTION

Much of the basis for the third major pattern of reactions to delinquency has already been discussed, and more research findings will be presented in this chapter. As we have seen, neither of the other broad perspectives on delinquency is adequate—although some of the specific lines of research and some of the action programs growing out of them continue to be valuable. The basic assumptions of the treatment and reform approaches, and to some extent even their goals, have been shown to be questionable. Perspectives described in the last chapter have—together with the additional findings and perspectives presented here—challenged the conventional wisdom of most delinquency research and policies. The approach I term "radical nonintervention" rests on a strikingly different set of core assumptions.

To begin with, we must repudiate the prevailing assumption that the delinquent is basically different. The "internal" types of individual difference do not provide a basis for explanation or a target for policy, nor do "external" sociocultural factors always act as causal variables. Delinquent acts do not somehow mysteriously appear for no good reason, but the kinds of causal variables that traditionally have dominated research provide at best only a very limited understanding of delinquency problems. So-called delinquents, in this view, are not significantly different from non-delinquents—*except* that they have been processed by the juvenile justice system. What they suffer from, more than either problems of the psyche or socioeconomic distress, is *contingencies*. Processing contingencies significantly shape delinquency rates, and in large measure also determine which specific individuals reach the various stages in the juvenile justice system. According to this outlook, a complete and accurate depiction of delinquency (processed *and* unprocessed) would reveal that most types of youthful misconduct are common within all socioeconomic strata in our society.

By the same token, the dominant conception of constraining forces, almost compelling individuals of certain sorts to become delinquent, requires, as Matza suggests, some revision. Conventional types of causal research can illuminate only selective and limited aspects of delinquency. The analysis of delinquency-producing interaction processes, by its new focus on reaction agencies, tell us more about delinquency than the analysis of variables that precipitate delinquent acts in individual cases. Similarly, the primary target for delinquency policy should be neither the individual nor the local community setting, but rather the delinquency-defining processes themselves.

We can now begin to see some of the meanings of the term "radical nonintervention." For one thing, it breaks radically with conventional thinking about delinquency and its causes. Basically, radical nonintervention implies policies that accommodate society to the widest possible diversity of behaviors and attitudes, rather than forcing as many individuals as possible to "adjust" to supposedly common societal standards. This does not mean that anything goes, that all behavior is socially acceptable. But traditional delinquency policy has proscribed youthful behavior well beyond what is required to maintain a smooth-running society or to protect others from youthful depredations.

Thus, the basic injunction for public policy becomes: *leave kids alone wherever possible.* This effort partly involves mechanisms to divert children away from the courts but it goes further to include opposing various kinds of intervention by diverse social control and socializing agencies. Radical nonintervention represents, perhaps, a more thoroughgoing and expanded version of the policy Lemert has termed "judicious nonintervention." [1] Subsidiary policies would favor collective action programs instead of those that single out specific individuals; and voluntary programs instead of compulsory ones. Finally, this approach is radical in asserting that major and intentional sociocultural change will help reduce our delinquency problems. Piecemeal socioeconomic reform will not greatly affect delinquency; there must be thoroughgoing changes in the structure and the values of our society. If the choice is between changing youth and changing the society (including some of its laws), the radical noninterventionist opts for changing the society.

THEORIES AND METHODS

Three specific bodies of research and theory have, along with the perspectives cited in the last chapter, encouraged and strengthened the radical nonintervention response: self-report studies that reveal much "hidden" delinquency; "control" and situational causation theories; and analyses of the possibly criminogenic features of juvenile justice and other social control processes. As we have seen, it has been widely assumed—as reform response strongly does—that delinquency is heavily concentrated among the lower classes. The radical nonintervention view, repudiating the notion that delinquents are basically different from nondelinquents, asserts in part that, on the contrary, delinquency is widespread among all segments of the society.

This is not a completely new idea. Sociologists have long been wary of official statistics, and several early studies showed that a great many cases of delinquency handled by private welfare agencies and in the schools never even came to the attention of the juvenile court.[2] Such research also revealed patterned variations in referral to the court—for example, older youths were more likely to be referred than younger ones and Negroes more than whites.[3] Close monitoring of the activities of individual youngsters, as in the Cambridge-Somerville Youth Study, similarly indicated that only a very small proportion of all acts of law-violation come to the attention of the authorities.[4]

SELF-REPORT TECHNIQUES. Perhaps the major breakthrough in studying this question, however, came with the development of "self-reported behavior" methods for exploring the distribution of delinquent acts. Researchers realized that if one wanted a true picture of the extent and distribution of law-violating behavior, it would be necessary to obtain data from samples drawn from the general population, instead of relying on the patently misrepresentative "samples" made up of persons who had been institutionalized or processed through the courts.

In early and somewhat rudimentary efforts along these lines, it was found that youngsters (and adults) were quite prepared to indicate the nature and extent of their past law violations when questioned by researchers in a straightforward and unthreatening way. Such investigations made clear that acts constituting crime or delinquency were extremely common and widespread, and also that there were striking socioeconomic differentials in the likelihood that official action would be taken against the offenders. Thus, in one of these studies it was found that a sample of college students had committed a great many offenses for which they could have been brought before the juvenile court, but unlike the nonstudents with whom they were compared, virtually none of them had been dealt with in this manner.[5] Since these pioneering efforts, a great deal of effort has been devoted to refining techniques for this kind of investigation, and a considerable body of data is now available.[6]

The relation between socioeconomic status and delinquency continues to preoccupy a good many sociologists, but no definitive thesis on the role of this element in delinquency causation has emerged. There has been a great deal of debate about the methodological soundness of even the more sophisticated self-report techniques; critics often maintain, in particular, that the "hidden" delinquency uncovered in these studies is relatively minor, whereas the more serious offenders are concentrated in the lower classes. They also argue that there probably is a great deal of hidden working-class delinquency. But it does seem clear that most youngsters do engage in acts that could be labeled delinquent, that only a small proportion of such acts are so labeled (i.e., officially processed and reported); and by and large there are substantial socio-economic differentials in the processing of delinquents. Furthermore, it is probably true that "not all of the hidden delinquency in the United States is petty and inconsequential. An indeterminate but important number of serious delinquencies is enacted by juveniles who manage to stay out of the hands of the police or courts." [7]

This does not mean that studies of lower-class delinquency are beside the point, or that a belief in the delinquency-generating effects of lower-class living conditions is untenable. These data do suggest, however, that delinquency-generating factors are also at work on a substantial scale among middle-class youth, and that an overall explanation must cope with this phenomenon as well.[8] Similarly, policies to improve the lot of lower-class youngsters may, if adopted on a sufficient scale, reduce the incidence of delinquent acts; but their impact on the diverse problems we term delinquency can only be limited. Thus, there is good reason to believe that social class simply is not *the* major factor that many recent formulations (notably, those influenced by reform outlooks) have made it out to be.

CONTROL THEORIES. Some of the efforts to explain delinquency causation in other than subcultural terms also further this line of argument. By and large, these can be grouped together, as Hirschi has done, as "control" theories.[9] In a way, Matza's "drift" conception is a prototype. The central idea behind all of these formulations is that delinquent behavior is often to be expected. One should try to explain its absence as well as its presence. According to these theories the persisting strength or the weakening (in particular situations) of *bonds to conventional society* makes the difference. From this standpoint, differences in delinquency *between* social classes are probably not as interesting as those *within* any class; the "control" element (whether it is called "containment," "commitment," or "attachment")[10] is crucial, whatever the individual's position in the social order. Of the approaches emphasizing social class, Hirschi comments: "While the prisons bulge with the socioeconomic dregs of society, careful quantitative research shows again and again that the relation between socioeconomic status and the commission of delinquent acts is small, or nonexistent."[11]

At first glance, it might seem that this approach represents a kind of reversion to the individual treatment outlook. There are some similarities between the two lines of analysis. Even though "control" theorists state the central research issue in an intriguingly new form ("The question 'Why do they do it' is simply not the question the theory is designed to answer. The question is 'Why don't we do it?' There is much evidence that we would if we dared."),[12] they are preoccupied with the traditional problem of distinguishing between offenders and nonoffenders (as determined, however, primarily through self-report data). Furthermore, the emphasis on bonds to conventional society as a key to "control" has resulted in renewed attention to the family, the school, and even religion. For example, findings in Hirschi's recent research suggested that

> . . . the closer the child's relations with his parents, the more he is attached to and identifies with them, the lower his chances of delinquency. It is argued here that the moral significance of this attachment resides directly in the attachment itself. The more strongly a child is attached to his parents, the more strongly he is bound to their expectations, and therefore the more strongly he is bound to conformity with the legal norms of the larger system.[13]

Similarly, the same author states with respect to school: "The boy who does not like school and who does not care what teachers think of him is to this extent free to commit delinquent acts. Positive feelings toward controlling institutions and persons in authority are the first line of social control. Withdrawal of favorable sentiments toward such institutions and persons at the same time neutralizes their moral force. Such neutralization is, in a control theory, a major link between lack of attachment and delinquency." [14]

For our purposes, however, the control thesis is most important because of the uniqueness of its conception of the delinquency-generating process. These processes are seen as open, fluid, and not fully determined, and provide considerable room for contingencies of social reaction to influence outcomes. Because "commitment" or "attachment" deters some youths from becoming delinquent, this approach reverses the idea of constraint. Instead of seeing some individuals as being constrained by individual or social forces, to commit delinquent acts, it emphasizes the ways bonds of conventionality constrain some individuals to remain law-abiding. This implies, furthermore, a new outlook on the role of values in promoting delinquency. Whereas earlier interpretations stressed the development of special, oppositional values that push lower-class youth into delinquency, here the emphasis is now on the common influence (in all classes) of dominant middle-class values. Individuals are not driven into delinquency by their frustration in achieving cultural goals; they are driven to it because their attachment to these goals has been *weakened* and *neutralized,* as shown by their various justifications of their behavior. [15] Unlike the oppositional subculture theories, this interpretation explains both lower- and middle-class delinquency in terms of roughly the same general process.

Along with their deemphasizing of delinquency-compelling subcultural values, control theorists also claim that the social structures within which delinquent acts occur are probably much less rigid than has been suggested by some of the analyses of gangs. This is supported by the earlier, controversial view that the gang is often no more than a "near-group": "The gang, in fact, had a shifting membership, no clarity as to what membership entailed, and individualized member images of gang size and function." [16] From this and similar analyses one can perceive a general picture of individuals who vary in their degree of attachment to conventional patterns and values, who are placed in situations where they might or might not engage in law violations, and who are thus open to a variety of situational forces including most significantly the reactions of other people with whom they are dealing. Thus, delinquency is seen as "the product of commitments to conformity, situationally induced motives to deviate, and a variety of contingencies." As the same writers go on to note, this framework "accounts for some aspects of this phenomena—such as its presence among most youth and its decline in early adulthood—which are not accounted for by other theoretical models." [17]

The fact that the control approach stresses mechanisms that cut across class lines and also operate within a given class doesn't mean that socioeconomic factors are irrelevant to delinquency causation. The following statement suggests how these general mechanisms and the social class system may be interrelated:

> . . . youngsters vary in the extent to which they feel a stake in American society. For those with social honor, disgrace is a powerful sanction. For a boy disapproved of already, there is less incentive to resist the temptation to do what he wants when he wants to do it. Usually, the higher the socioeconomic status of the family, the more the youngster feels he has to lose by deviant behavior. . . . To determine the stake which a youngster has in conformity, it is necessary to know more than the level which his family occupies in the economic system. His own victories and defeats in interpersonal relations can be predicted only roughly from family income or father's occupation. [18]

SOCIAL CONTROL PROCESSES. The final strand of analysis underpinning the radical nonintervention response focuses on possible delinquency-promoting features of juvenile justice and other social control processes. As we have seen, labeling studies—of the police, probation officers, and the juvenile court—show how stereotyping, retrospective interpretation, and negotiation, as well as the organization's own needs, influence the selection of individuals for official processing and the disposition of the cases. The system itself, in terms of these selection processes alone, must be recognized as "producing" delinquency. Less well documented are the specific, long-term effects of such processes—in particular their impact on youthful self-concepts and delinquent careers.

In his book *Delinquency and Drift*, Matza argues that the juvenile justice system promotes delinquency in a much broader sense than simply by selecting out individual offenders. As we saw earlier, he claims that the court hearing induces confusion and distrust among those exposed to it. Beyond that, he asserts, the juvenile court process creates an overpowering *sense of injustice* among youths who come before it or learn about it indirectly, and thus it strengthens rather than combats delinquency-generating attitudes. Matza states:

> The major meanings of fairness are captured, I believe in the following assertions: it is only fair that some steps be taken to ascertain whether I was really the wrongdoer (cognizance); it is only fair that I be treated according to the same principles as others of my status (consistency); it is only fair that you who pass judgment on me sustain the right to do so (competence); it is only fair that some relationship obtain between the magnitude of what I have done and what you propose to do to me (commensurability); it is only fair that differences between the treatment of my status and others be reasonable and tenable (comparison). Each of these statements poses an elementary component of justice.[19]

According to Matza, youths processed by the traditional juvenile court have good reason to feel that their treatment violates these basic criteria of fairness or justice. The proceeding is vague and inconsistent, and perhaps, in the eyes of some beholders, hypocritical and incompetent. It is hardly surprising then, Matza contends, if most youths judge those passing judgment in terms as harsh as those applied to themselves, and condemn the entire system of supposed "justice," which represents, in the youth's eyes, middle-class society.

While Matza's interpretation was based largely on general observation rather than on "hard" data, his argument makes sense in terms of what we do know about both youthful attitudes and the workings of the juvenile justice mechanisms. Findings from more recent empirical studies are inconclusive. In general, the argument that the court experience creates confusion seems to be valid. As we noted earlier, the organization of the juvenile justice system is very complex; it reflects a multiplicity of goals, conflicting interests, and the tensions between personnel with highly varying personal backgrounds and social and professional attitudes: The following statement is by a judge who is involved in juvenile work:

> There has been a complete breakdown in communications be-
> tween the personnel who work in juvenile court—breakdown be-
> tween judges and social workers, between social workers and psy-
> chiatrists, between the probation officers and all these groups,
> and the juvenile officers . . .—a breakdown in communication
> between the parties representing the various disciplines that ap-
> pear in the juvenile courts.[20]

Interviews with children who actually have gone through the court procedure indicate that it is very difficult for them to understand what is going on. A recent research report quoted the following as typical of such reactions:

> I couldn't understand anything he said. The only thing I under-
> stood was "you're committed." Everything else was a bunch of
> mumble-jumble. He went on and on a mile a minute and you
> sit there twiddling your thumbs and waiting for what he says
> . . . you're just listening for the main word, you're either com-
> mitted or you're going home. You don't listen to that other stuff.
> They just said they didn't want to send me here [the Reception
> Center, where the interview occurred], that they didn't want to
> do it, that's all. I thought that was a bunch of baloney that they
> didn't want to send me here.[21]

In a related study, processed delinquents expressed extremely nega-
tive feelings about the entire court experience, although at the same time they did not claim that they had been unfairly treated.[22] These reactions probably vary a great deal from court to court, and from judge to judge. One investigation has indicated that the child's sense of participation in the proceedings (especially the extent to which he is allowed to speak) greatly influences his evaluation of the proceedings.[23]

THE SCHOOLS. This double critique—focusing both on specific labeling processes and on broader questions of the entire system's legitimacy—has been aimed at another major agency of social control over youth, the schools. The treatment orientation considers the schools as control agencies that can effectively identify potential

delinquents and provide them with special counseling. The liberal reformists emphasize equality of educational opportunity, adequacy of school conditions, and educational programs that take into account cultural (class, racial, and ethnic) heterogeneity. The radical noninterventionist would point out the ways in which schools promote delinquency by early labeling of kids as troublemakers, and would question the legitimacy of the educational system's goals as well as its means.

Much of the labeling that occurs in schools varies according to the outlooks and practices adopted by individual teachers. The teacher is always in a crucial position to shape the student's course of development:

> . . . what is made of an act depends almost entirely on how it is defined and evaluated by the teacher, including the issue of whether or not the act is a violation of the basic authority rule. The boy is using the teacher to define himself as autonomous, and, like his behavior on the streets, he often creates or provokes the situation in which he then defends his honor. Yet if a teacher is willing to concede the fact that school is meaningless to some boys and therefore that other activities besides "teaching and learning" will necessarily go on in class, and if he is willing to limit the scope of his jurisdiction to the activity of "teaching and learning" itself, then his authority is likely to remain intact, regardless of how much it may be "tested." Whether or not he wishes to persuade the boys to join the learning process is another matter. . . .[24]

All too often, unfortunately, an overriding concern with matters other than "teaching and learning" has meant that, "the balance has traditionally been on the side of debasement, exclusion, and locking out, rather than on the side of respect, reinvolvement, and recommitment of the misbehaving student."[25] Narrow conceptions regarding the potential learning capacities of large numbers of students, and individualistic and moralistic outlooks on disruptive behavior, abet this tendency.

Such processes, however, are not simply a result of the misguided efforts of individual teachers. Both the structure and the goals of the school system are heavily implicated. Unintended consequences of the so-called "tracking" or ability-grouping systems now employed so widely in our schools are particularly noteworthy. This procedure, by definition a labeling process, is almost bound to have undesirable social psychological side-effects. These dangers have been revealed by recent experimental research in which students' IQ scores and grades directly varied according to the nature of the information about their "prospects" provided to their teachers.[26] One analysis of tracking concludes that "if, as often claimed, American teachers underestimate the learning potential of low-track students and expect more negative attitudes and greater trouble from them, it may well be that they partially cause the very failure, alienation, lack of involvement, dropping out, and rebellion they are seeking to prevent." [27] Closely related to the tracking system are the activities of school counselors, recently subjected to an intensive sociological analysis. According to the authors of that study:

> In a bureaucratically organized school such as Lakeshore High, the classification of students routinely initiates organizational actions that may progressively define and limit the development of such [student] careers. From this perspective, the criteria employed in the evaluation process, the information considered relevant and recorded, the interpretations made of such information, and the organizationally defined categories by which students are classified are important for an understanding of how the school produces senior students who are or are not qualified for college entrance, "highly recommended" or "poor prospects," "well-rounded personalities" or "maladjusted." [28]

As those writers also point out, the "organizational emphasis upon talent and the pursuit of narrow specialties" imposes on children in all tracks the need to make very early decisions and affords little opportunity to explore fully a range of possible interests and abilities.[29]

Increasingly, these selection and labeling processes begin very early in the school careers of children, and display a largely cumulative course. The self-fulfilling nature of such labeing is difficult for the child to reverse or overcome, and school records (both of academic work and of other behavior patterns) are, like hospital or court records, reinforced by the process of retrospective interpretation. These records follow the child throughout his school career and significantly affect the options open to him at various stages. In this sense, then, the schools—like the police and the courts—help produce "delinquents."

Basic goals of the school system also are being questioned in various analyses of youth problems. Beyond the enforced cultural assimilation to white middle-class values and norms that even the reformists might condemn radical critics contend that the educational system must be challenged for socializing youngsters to live as members of what they see as a morally bankrupt way of life. The schools have become one more example (along with prisons and "training schools") of the self-alienating bureaucratic "total institutions" that dominate technocratic society. From all of these standpoints, it is questionable whether the schools—even when they are efficiently and fairly administered and staffed—are likely to meet the real needs of young people. An argument has long been made that schools may not be for everybody, that to some extent continued schooling represents an unwanted exclusion from adult responsibility, and that alternatives to compulsory schooling for older youths ought be given more serious consideration.[30] Currently, radical educationists attribute many if not most of our social ills to compulsory schooling, and argue for a general "deschooling" of society. One of the major spokesmen for this position, Ivan Illich, asserts:

> If we do not challenge the assumption that valuable knowledge is a commodity which under certain circumstances may be forced into the consumer, society will be increasingly dominated by sinister pseudo-schools and totalitarian managers of information. Pedagogical therapists will drug their pupils more in order to teach them better, and students will drug themselves more to gain relief from the pressures of teachers and the race for certificates.[31]

This is well confirmed by developing tendencies in the treatment of, and reactions by, American youth.

TOWARD NEW PRIORITIES

Do all the accumulated data from earlier research and the new perspectives in delinquency analysis provide us any guidelines for public policy? One point seems very clear: there is no single program that constitutes *the* solution to problems of youthful misconduct, nor can we realistically expect one to emerge suddenly. There is not even a readily identifiable combination of programs that would quickly and effectively reduce delinquency on a broad scale. However, there is a lesson to be learned from the process by which we reach that conclusion. Our energies and commitment ought no longer to be squandered in a futile search for simplistic answers, either in public policy or in "causal theory." There is no point in arguing endlessly about whether detached worker programs are better than guided group interaction schemes, just as there is only limited benefit to be derived from determining the exact social psychological mechanisms that lead individual children into delinquent behavior.

Furthermore, while it is apparent that many of the present programs do have some real but limited value, the processes by which particular programs are selected in the various jurisdictions reflect more than just rational assessment according to established criteria of effectiveness. Organizational need and vested interest, and the conflicting general perspectives on delinquency and juvenile justice necessarily influence policy-making in this field. Not that there is no room for rational planning. An enormous number of highly specific policies are now being chosen; obviously, the greatest possible wisdom should be brought to bear on these decisions. However, what is most needed at this juncture is a very broad perspective that can guide policy-making at all levels. Certain general conclusions and broad lines of priority immediately suggest themselves.

1. THERE IS NEED FOR A THOROUGH REASSESSMENT OF THE DOMINANT WAYS OF THINKING ABOUT YOUTH "PROBLEMS." We can no longer afford the comforting illusion that these problems are com-

pletely attributable to identifiable individuals—whether we label them "bad," "sick," or "socially disadvantaged." The behavior patterns in question are part and parcel of our social and cultural system, and any efforts to change them must take that centrally into account. Youthful "misconduct," like misconduct generally, is inevitable under any form of social order. There is some leeway to influence the extent and forms of misconduct that prevail under a particular set of social conditions, but this influence can only operate as a consequence of efforts to shape the broader sociocultural and definitional contexts that the behavior reflects. From this standpoint the specific youth "problems" we now experience have to be recognized as one of the prices we pay for maintaining a particular kind of social structure and dominant value system. We have to consider whether it is worth paying the price. We may conclude on sober reflection that we have greatly and unnecessarily exaggerated the price; that we accept some of this behavior instead of considering it socially problematic and trying to "solve" it by legal methods. In some instances, we may feel that the price paid is so high and so alarming that major changes in our social and cultural systems are necessary.

2. SOME OF THE MOST VALUABLE POLICIES FOR DEALING WITH DELINQUENCY ARE NOT NECESSARILY THOSE DESIGNATED AS DELINQUENCY POLICIES. This follows from the fact that delinquency reflects more general sociocultural conditions. Yet, as I stated in the first chapter, we "compartmentalize" crime and delinquency phenomena. Somehow, when we try to remake our socioeconomic order and reshape our dominant cultural values, we do not feel that we are confronting the specifically disturbing behavior we call delinquency. The impact of such efforts must be indirect, and perhaps incomplete, but we would do well to heed the following recent comment: "the construction of a just system of criminal justice in an unjust society is a contradiction in terms." [32] Since delinquency and juvenile justice are in some degree inherently political phenomena, major changes in this area necessarily require broad political decisions.

3. WE MUST TAKE YOUNG PEOPLE MORE SERIOUSLY IF WE ARE TO ERADICATE INJUSTICE TO JUVENILES. There is some evidence that the

most potent deterrent to delinquency lies in bonds of attachment to conventional society. Perhaps we should concentrate more on strengthening those bonds than on combating "criminogenic" forces that supposedly have a hold on our children. This, in turn, implies not only the creation of a more just and egalitarian society, but also a legal system that young people can respect, and above all, a sense among young people that the society respects them. It is not necessary that we all join the counterculture. But our acceptance of cultural pluralism (as in racial and ethnic matters) must also govern our attitudes and policies toward youth. Our traditional reactions to youth and our definitions of youth problems have been very ambivalent—fear and envy mixed with admiration and fond concern.[33] Indeed, the fact that adults see youth as a "problem" reflects this outlook. Sane youth policies will have to be based on greater acceptance of young people on their own terms, a willingness to live with a variety of life styles, and a recognition of the fact that the young people of our society are not necessarily confused, troubled, sick, or vicious. These attitudes cannot emerge within the context of the present juvenile justice system, with its paternalistic, patronizing, even hostile philosophy.

4. THE JUVENILE JUSTICE SYSTEM SHOULD CONCERN ITSELF LESS WITH THE PROBLEMS OF SO-CALLED "DELINQUENTS," AND MORE WITH DISPENSING JUSTICE. A major first step in this direction would be to greatly narrow the present jurisdiction of the juvenile court. It is significant that even the President's Crime Commission, a far from "radical" body, has made such a recommendation: "in view of the serious stigma and the uncertain gain accompanying official action, serious consideration should be given complete elimination from the court's jurisdiction of conduct illegal only for a child." [34] But beyond this, the entire conception of "individualized justice" requires reassessment. In combination with the vagueness of delinquency statutes, the enormous amount of discretion vested in officials at the various stages of delinquency-processing invites uncertainty and confusion and sets the stage for discriminatory practices. Nor does the basic notion of 'treating" the child's broad problems, rather than reacting to a specific law violation, appear to further the aim of "rehabilitation" in any meaningful way. In

fact the sense of injustice to which this approach gives rise may, as we have seen, actively reinforce attitudes that breed delinquency. The authors of *Struggle for Justice* are right when they insist:

> The whole person is not the concern of the law. Whenever the law considers the whole person, it is more likely that it considers factors irrelevant to the purpose of delivering punishment. The other factors, by and large, have been and will certainly continue to be characteristics related to influence, power, wealth, and class. They will not be factors related to the needs or the treatment potentialities of the defendant.[35]

Individualized justice must necessarily give way to a *return to the rule of law*. This means that while fewer types of youthful behavior will be considered legal offenses, in cases of really serious misconduct such traditional guidelines as *specificity, uniformity,* and *nonretroactivity* ought apply. Juvenile statutes should spell out very clearly just what kinds of behavior are legally proscribed, and should set explicit penalties for such violations (with perhaps some limited range of alternatives available to sentencing judges). This is quite consistent with what research has told us about the nature of delinquency causation and the efficacy of treatment, and carries the great advantage that it would increase clarity, ensure more equitable administration of justice, and would probably generate among young people greater respect for the legal system. Such measures would not constitute a "get tough" policy so much as a "deal evenly" one, and—it should again be emphasized—they would apply to a much narrower range of "offenses" than now exists. For those kinds of behavior that society is reluctant to simply "do nothing about," but for which a stern legal approach seems inappropriate, various "diversion" schemes such as those cited earlier could be developed.

These policies would squarely face up to the euphemistic evasions that have characterized much of juvenile "justice" in the past, and they would state premises and goals candidly and decisively. It is not heartlessly conservative to recognize that there may be certain actions we wish to punish, provided the range of offenses is carefully circumscribed and the rules equitably administered. But most of the stern measures taken against young people have not been in their "best interests." Continuing to delude ourselves on that score can only impede the development of sane delinquency policy.

5. AS JUVENILE JUSTICE MOVES IN NEW DIRECTIONS, A VARIETY OF APPROACHES WILL CONTINUE TO BE USEFUL. Even if enough people with the power to effect legislative and judicial change become convinced that an entirely new approach along the lines I have indicated is needed, it will take time to reach that goal. While the system is moving in that direction (and I have tried to show that it already is), certain understandings that already are beginning to be part of the "conventional wisdom" in the delinquency field might well guide policy. With respect to prevention programs those with a collective or community focus should be preferred to those that single out and possibly stigmatize particular individuals. Programs that employ "indigenous" personnel (local community people such as older youths who have been gang members) should be preferred to those that employ only outside professionals. As regards treatment, noninstitutional and voluntary programs should be preferred over institutional and compulsory ones, and most likely the ultimate goal should be the abolition of treatment institutions as such.[36] In the meantime, available evidence favors emphasizing relatively unstructured group sessions more than intensive individual psychotherapy. Bureaucratic and identity-destroying features should be eliminated in existing institutions, and practical training that can be useful on return to the outside world should be stressed.

These priorities, however, do not really get to the heart of the matter—which is the overall perspective that guides our thinking about youth and delinquency. As the dominant reactions change, specific policy priorities are bound to change with them. That this process is now actively underway is due, in some measure, to the efforts of sociologists and other researchers to penetrate the surface appearances and stated philosophy of juvenile justice—to get beyond the law on the books and show us the law in action. By focusing on major reaction patterns, we can see the interrelationship between premise and policy. In their interminable search for "causes," sociologists have produced no definitive "solution" to delinquency problems. They have, however, alerted us to many misconceptions and blind alleys, and begun to show us the direction that policy might sensibly take. Our young people deserve something better than being "processed." Hopefully, we are beginning to realize this.

✠ ✠ ✠

1. Edwin M. Lemert, "The Juvenile Court—Quest and Realities," in President's Commission on Law Enforcement and Administration of Justice, *Task Force Report: Juvenile Delinquency and Youth Crime* (Washington, D.C.: U.S. Government Printing Office, 1967), pp. 96–97.

2. Sophia M. Robison, *Can Delinquency Be Measured?* (New York: Columbia University Press, 1936); Edward E. Schwartz, "A Community Experiment in the Measurement of Delinquency," *Yearbook*, National Probation Association, 1945, pp. 157–81.

3. For a more recent study analyzing court referrals by the police, see Nathan Goldman, *The Differential Selection of Juvenile Offenders for Court Appearance* (New York: National Council on Crime and Delinquency, 1963).

4. Fred J. Murphy, Mary M. Shirley, and Helen L. Witmer, "The Incidence of Hidden Delinquency," *American Journal of Orthopsychiatry*, 16 (October, 1946), 686–95.

5. Austin L. Porterfield, *Youth in Trouble* (Ft. Worth, Texas: Leo Potishman Foundation, 1946).

6. See, for example, James F. Short and F. Ivan Nye, "Reported Behavior as a Criterion of Deviant Behavior," *Social Problems*, 5 (Winter, 1957–58), 207–213; and "Extent of Unrecorded Juvenile Delinquency: Tentative Conclusions," *Journal of Criminal Law, Criminology, and Police Science*, 49 (November–December, 1958), 296–302; also Maynard L. Erickson and LaMar Empey, "Court Records, Undetected Delinquency, and Decision-Making," *Journal of Criminal Law, Criminology, and Police Science*, 54 (December, 1963), 456–69; Harwin L. Voss, "Socioeconomic Status and Reported Delinquent Behavior," *Social Problems*, 13 (Winter, 1966), 314–24; and Leroy C. Gould, "Who Defines Delinquency," *Social Problems*, 16 (Winter, 1969), 325–35.

7. Don C. Gibbons, *Delinquent Behavior* (Englewood Cliffs, N.J.: Prentice-Hall, Inc., 1970), p. 31.

8. For a variety of perspectives on this matter, see Edmund W. Vaz, ed., *Middle-Class Juvenile Delinquency* (New York: Harper & Row, Publishers, 1967).

9. Travis Hirschi, *Causes of Delinquency* (Berkeley: University of California Press, 1969).

10. See, for example, Walter C. Reckless, "A New Theory of Delinquency and Crime," in Rose Giallombardo, ed., *Juvenile Delinquency* (New York: John Wiley & Sons, Inc., 1966); Larry Karacki and Jackson Toby, "The Uncommitted Adolescent: Candidate for Gang Socialization," *Sociological Inquiry*, 32 (Spring, 1962), 203–215; also, Reiss, "Delinquency as the Failure of Personal and Social Controls"; and Hirschi, *Causes of Delinquency*.

11. Hirschi, *Causes of Delinquency*, p. 66.

12. *Ibid.*, p. 34.

13. *Ibid.*, p. 94; see also Nye, *Family Relationships and Delinquent Behavior*.

14. Hirschi, *Causes of Delinquency*, p. 127; see also Arthur L. Stinchcombe, *Rebellion in a High School* (Chicago: Quadrangle Books, 1964); and Kenneth Polk and David Halferty, "School Cultures, Adolescent Commitments, and Delinquency," in Kenneth Polk and Walter E. Schafer, eds. *Schools and Delinquency* (Englewood Cliffs, N.J.: Prentice-Hall, 1972), pp. 71–90.

15. See Gresham Sykes and David Matza, "Techniques of Neutralization: A Theory of Delinquency," *American Sociological Review*, 22 (December, 1957), 664–70; David Matza, *Delinquency and Drift* (New York: John Wiley & Sons, Inc., 1964); also Matza and Sykes, "Juvenile Delinquency and Subterranean Values," *American Sociological Review*, 26 (Oct. 1961), pp. 712–19.

16. Lewis Yablonsky, "The Delinquent Gang as a Near-Group," *Social Problems*, 2 (Fall, 1959), pp. 108–117, as reprinted in Giallombardo, *Juvenile Delinquency*, p. 254; see also Howard L. and Barbara G. Myerhoff, "Field Observations of Middle Class 'Gangs,'" *Social Forces* (March, 1964), pp. 328–36.

17. Scott Briar and Irving Piliavin, "Delinquency, Situational Inducements, and Commitment to Conformity," *Social Problems*, 13 (Summer, 1965), p. 45; see also James F. Short, Jr., and Fred L. Strodtbeck, *Group Process and Gang Delinquency* (Chicago: University of Chicago Press, 1965).

18. Jackson Toby, "Social Disorganization and Stake in Conformity: Complementary Factors in the Predatory Behavior of Hoodlums," *Journal of Criminal Law, Criminology and Police Science*, 48 (1957), pp. 12–17, as reprinted in Daniel Glaser, ed., *Crime in the City* (New York: Harper & Row, 1970), p. 136.

19. David Matza, *Delinquency and Drift*, p. 106.

20. Quoted in Wheeler, Bonacich, Cramer, and Zola, "Agents of

Delinquency Control: A Comparative Analysis," in Wheeler, ed., *Controlling Delinquents* (New York: John Wiley & Sons, 1968), pp. 33–34.

21. Quoted in Martha Baum and Stanton Wheeler, "Becoming an Inmate," in Wheeler, ed., *Controlling Delinquents*, p. 166.

22. Brendan Maher, with Ellen Stein, "The Delinquent's Perception of the Law and the Community," *ibid.*

23. Paul D. Lipsitt, "The Juvenile Offender's Perceptions," *Crime and Delinquency*, 14 (January, 1968), 49–62.

24. Carl Werthman, "The Function of Social Definitions in the Development of Delinquent Careers," in President's Commission on Law Enforcement and Administration of Justice, *Task Force Report: Juvenile Delinquency and Youth Crime*, p. 166.

25. Walter E. Schafer and Kenneth Polk, "Delinquency and the Schools," *ibid.*, p. 234.

26. Robert Rosenthal and Lenore Jacobson, *Pygmalion in the Classroom* (New York: Holt, Rinehart & Winston, Inc., 1968).

27. Walter E. Schafer, Carol Olexa, and Kenneth Polk, "Programmed for Social Class: Tracking in High School," in Polk and Schafer, *Schools and Delinquency*, pp. 46–47.

28. Aaron V. Cicourel and John I. Kitsuse, *The Educational Decision-Makers* (Indianapolis, Ind.: The Bobbs-Merrill Company, Inc., 1963), p. 75.

29. *Ibid.*, p. 146.

30. F. Musgrove, *Youth and the Social Order* (Bloomington: Indiana University Press, 1965).

31. Ivan Illich, *Deschooling Society*, Harrow Books (New York: Harper & Row, Publishers, 1972), p. 72.

32. *Struggle for Justice*, p. 16.

33. See Edgar Z. Friedenberg, *The Vanishing Adolescent*, Laurel Books (New York: Dell Publishing Company, 1962).

34. President's Commission on Law Enforcement and Administration of Justice, *Task Force Report: Juvenile Delinquency and Youth Crime*, p. 27.

35. *Struggle for Justice*, p. 147.

36. See Homer Bigart, "Alternatives to Reformatories Hailed Amid Controversy in Massachusetts," *The New York Times*, September 1, 1972, p. 8.

Index

Action research, 4–5
American Friends Service Committee: *Struggle for Justice*, 127–28, 142–43, 146–47
Annandale experiment, 68–69
Anomie theory, of delinquency, 17, 85, 91
Area analysis, 15
Ascribed status, 120
Assault, acts of, 13
Austin, David M.: "Gang Workers," 98
Autobiography, use of, 84, 138
Aversive suppression, 52

Barron, Milton L.: *Juvenile in Delinquent Society*, 108
Becker, Howard S.: *Outsiders*, 39, 118
Behavior modification, 51–64
Biological theories, of delinquency, 31–34
Bureaucratization, 130–35

California Youth Authority, 4, 18, 60–61, 63
Cambridge-Somerville Youth Study, 46–48, 54–55, 156
Case histories, use of, 14, 122–25 (*see also* Autobiographies)
Chein, Isidor: *Road to H*, 85–86
Chicago Area Project, 84–89, 102, 103–5
Child-rearing practices, 45
Cicourel, Aaron:
  Educational Decision-Makers, 164
  Juvenile Justice, 124
Circumstantial vulnerability, principle of, 49
Class differences, and delinquency, 42–43, 82, 89ff., 92–94, 156–57
Clinics, child-guidance, 56
Cloward, R. A., and L. E. Ohlin: *Delinquency and Opportunity*, 90–93, 102
Cohen, Albert K.:

Cohen, Albert K. (*Cont.*)
  Delinquent Boys, 42–43, 89–90, 92, 110
  Deviance and Control, 39–40, 137–38
Community programs:
  for individual treatment, 58–63
  and the reform response, 102–5
Compulsory treatment, 23
Concentric zone theory, 84–85
Connor, Walter: *Deviance in Soviet Society*, 108–9
Constraint, idea of, 30, 135–36
Control theories, 157–60
Cottage parents, in institutions, 66–67
Council of the Society for the Psychological Study of Social Issues, 50
Counseling, and individual treatment, 54–57
Counterculture, and delinquency, 140–43
Courts: (*see also* Laws)
  and confusion, juvenile sense of, 161–62
  Gault decision, 4, 129
  and "individualized justice," 168–69
  and individual treatment, 70–71
  and injustice, juvenile sense of, 161
  judges, 47–48
  juvenile contempt for, 129–30
  and labeling, 118–26
  negotiation in, 123–26
  organizational analysis of, 132–35
  paternalism of, 107–8
  and the police, 133
  radical noninterventionist recommendations for, 168–71
  and the reform response, 110–11
  and "socialized justice," 128–29
Cultural transmission theory, of delinquency, 17

Delinquency: (*see also* Individual treatment; Reformist response; Radical nonintervention)
  and the counterculture, 140–43
  definitions of, 5–6
  deterministic theories of, 30–31, 135–39
  and euphemism, use of, 126–30
  as an external phenomenon, 10–11
  and individual treatment, 19, 20–24, 29–71
  interactionist views of, 17, 40, 136–38
  labeling of, 6, 23, 50, 118–26, 133
  and liberal reform, 19, 20–24
  and the mass media, 11–12, 109–10
  and middle-class values, 90
  and neo-antideterminism, 135–39
  normative issues of, 6–7
  organizational management of, 130–35
  patterned reactions to, 19–23
  and peer values, 59, 68–69, 86–87, 93
  as a political phenomenon, 139–43
  prediction of, 46–51
  proneness to, 122
  psychological theories of, 34–41
  public beliefs concerning, 9–13
  and radical nonintervention, 19, 20–24, 153–71
  reform responses to, 81–111
  and social bonds, 157–59, 167–68
  and social class differences, 42–43, 82, 89ff., 92–94, 156–57
  and social conditions, 81–111
  sociological theories of, 9, 18, 19, 38–39, 41–43
  subcultures of, 89–90
  theories of, 16–17

traditions of, 87–88
typologies of, 13–17
in the U.S.S.R., 108–9
and will, role of, 138–39
Deterministic theories, of delinquency, 30–31, 135–39
Deviance, labeling of, 118–26
Devlin, Lord Patrick, 143–44
Differential association, concept of, 87–88
Diversion proposals, and individual treatment, 61–63
Drift, concept of, 136
Drug addiction, 35–36, 85–86, 91–92
  compulsory treatment of, 129
  sociological theories of, 42
  as a victimless crime, 144–45
Drugs, behavior-modifying, 51–52
Durkheim, Emile, 89

Ecological theories, of delinquency, 41–42, 84–85
Electronic monitoring, 52, 53
Emerson, Robert M.: *Judging Delinquents,* 132–33
Erikson, Kai T.: "Sociology of Deviance," 120
Euphemism, use of, 126–30
"Evil causes evil," fallacy of, 11, 83, 108, 123

Factor analysis, 85
Family influences, 43–45
  female-based households, 42–43, 93
Ferdinand, Theodore N.: *Typologies of Delinquency,* 13, 14
Financial success, and American society, 89–90
Flacks, Richard: *Youth and Social Change,* 141–42

Gangs, 87
  and the mass media, 11–12
  and the reform response, 94–101

Garfinkel, Harold: "Degradation Ceremonies," 121–22
Gault case, of the Supreme Court, 4, 129
Gibbons, Don C.:
  Changing the Lawbreaker, 15–16
  Delinquent Behavior, 31, 33, 36
Girls Vocational High Study, 55
Glueck, Sheldon and Eleanor:
  Physique and Delinquency, 33–34
  Unraveling Juvenile Delinquency, 43–44, 49–50
Goffman, Erving: *Asylums,* 122–23, 130
Goodman, Paul: *Growing Up Absurd,* 141
Gottfredson, Don M.: "Assessment and Prediction Methods," 48
Group interaction, 59, 68–69, 170

Hart, H. L. A., 144
Henthoff, Nat: "Drug-Pushing in the Schools," 52
Highfields (N.J.) experiment, 68–69
Hirschi, Travis:
  Causes of Delinquency, 17, 157, 158–59
  and Selvin, Hanan C.: *Delinquency Research,* 34, 44

Identity-stripping, 121–22
Illich, Ivan: *Deschooling Society,* 165
Incorrigibility, 119
Individual treatment, 19, 20–24, 29–71
  behavior modification, 51–64
  biological theories, 31–34
  and community programs, 58–63
  and counseling, 54–57
  and the courts, 70–71
  differentness, assumption of, 11, 29–31

Individual treatment (*Cont.*)
  diversion proposals, 61–63
  family influences, 43–45
  in institutions, 64–71
  and probation, 57–58
  psychological theories of, 34–41
  sociological theories of, 41–43, 82–83
Institutions: (*see also* Rehabilitation)
  cottage parents in, 66–67
  and individual treatment, 64–71
  inmate norms and sanctions, 65
  innovations in, 67–68
  organizational analysis of, 130–35
  professionals vs. nonprofessionals, 66–67
  rehabilitation in, 65–66, 69–70
  schools, 162–65
Interactionist views, of delinquency, 17, 40, 118–26, 136–38
Interpersonal Maturity Level Classification, 60

Judges, 47–48 (*see also* Courts)
Juvenile Delinquency (*see* Delinquency)

Kanter, David, and W. I. Bennett: "Street-Corner Workers," 96–97
Kinds-of-people comparisons, 37, 41
Klein, Malcolm W.: *Street Gangs and Street Workers*, 12, 94–95, 99–100
Knight, Doug: *Delinquency Causes and Remedies*, 4, 18
Kobrin, Solomon: "Chicago Area Project," 103

Labeling, of delinquency, 6, 23, 50, 118–26, 133

and the courts, 118–26
and negotiation, 123–26
retrospective interpretation, 121–23
in the schools, 164–65
stereotyping, 120–21
Lander, Bernard: *Understanding Juvenile Delinquency*, 85
Latent delinquency, 39
Laws, on delinquency, 7, 8 (*see also* Courts)
  conservative reactions of, 19, 21
  vs. private morality, 143–44
  sociologists' interpretations of, 9
  and victimless crimes, 144–45
Lemert, Edwin:
  Human Deviance, 126
  Instead of Court, 62, 63
  "Juvenile Court," 155
Lerman, Paul: "Institutions for Delinquents," 61
Liberal reform, 19, 20–24
Lindesmith, Alfred R.: "Drug Addict as Psychopath," 35–36
Lower classes, and delinquency, 92–94

McCord, William and Joan: *Psychopath*, 34–35, 37
McCorkle, L. W., et al.: *Highfields Story*, 68–69
Mannheim, Hermann: *Criminal Justice*, 9
Martin, John M., et al.: *Analysis of Delinquent Behavior*, 14–15, 17, 142
Mass media:
  and cultural values, 109–10
  and street gangs, 11–12
  and television violence, 109–10
Maternal deprivation, 43–44
Maturity levels, classification by, 60–61
Matza, David:
  Becoming Deviant, 138–39

Delinquency and Drift, 30, 37–38, 81–82, 129, 135–36, 154, 157, 160–61

Merton, Robert K.: "Social Structure and Anomie," 89, 92, 109

Mesomorphy, 33

Midcity Youth Project, 96–97, 100–101, 133–34

Miller, Walter:
"Lower Class Culture," 92–94, 100–101
"Theft Behavior," 13

Minnesota Multiphasic Personality Test, 46

Mobilization for Youth (New York City), 102–3

National Training School for Boys (Washington, D.C.), 52

Negotiation, in the courts, 123–26

Negroes:
stigmatizing of, 125–26
vs. white norms, 142, 143

Neo-antideterminism, 135–39

Neurological learning-disability syndrome, 32–33

New York City Youth Board Study, 46–47, 49–51

New York Times, The, 32–33

Normal, concept of, 37

Operant conditioning, 52–53

Organizational analysis:
and institutions, 130–35
and vested interests, 134–35

Packer, Herbert, 145, 146

Parens patriae, concept of, 70

Parsons, Talcott, 42–43

Passaic Children's Bureau, 62

Peer values, influence of, 59, 68–69, 86–87, 93

Piliavin, Irving, and Scott Brian: "Police Encounters," 121

Pinehills (Utah) program, 59–60

Platt, Anthony M.: *Child Savers*, 3, 21, 119

Plea bargaining, 123

Polsky, Howard W.: *Cottage Six*, 65

Poverty, war on, 106–7

Powers, E., and H. Witmer: *Prevention of Delinquency*, 54

Predelinquency, 39, 46–51, 71

President's Commission on Law Enforcement, 5, 57, 58, 63, 105, 132, 168

Probation, 57–58
officers, 131, 132–33

Psychiatry, social work in, 57–58
and gangs, 100–101

Psychological theories, of delinquency, 16, 17, 34–41
and childhood, 37–38

Psychopathic personality, 34–36

Radical nonintervention, 19, 20–24, 153–71
assumptions of, 153–54
and control theories, 157–60
and the courts, 168–71
and the schools, 162–65
self-report techniques, 156–57
and social control processes, 160–62
theories and methods of, 155–66

Reform responses, to delinquency, 81–111
and community programs, 102–5
and cultural values, 109
and general social reform, 105–10
and socialized justice, 110–11
theories and methods of, 84–94

Rehabilitation:
as a euphemism, 127–30
in institutions, 65–66, 69–70

Retrospective interpretation, 121–23

Rodman, Hyman, and Paul Grams: "Juvenile Delinquency and the Family," 44–45

Ryan, William: *Blaming the Victim,* 107

Schools:
labeling processes in, 164–65
radical noninterventionist critiques of, 162–65

Schwitzgebel, Ralph K.: *Behavior Modification Techniques,* 52–53

Self-report techniques, 156–57

Shaw, Clifford R.: *Delinquency Areas,* 84–85, 87

Situational analysis, 14–15

Social bonds, and delinquency, 157–59, 167–68

Social classes, 42–43, 92–94, 156–57
and rates of delinquency, 82, 89ff.

Societal reactions, analysis of, 118–26

Sociological theories, of delinquency, 9, 16–19, 38–39, 41–43
and drug addiction, 42
"evil causes evil," fallacy of, 11, 83, 108, 123
and individual treatment, 41–43, 82–83
kinds-of-people comparisons, 37, 41

Sociopathic personality, 36

Stanfield, Robert E., and Brendan Mahler: "Clinical and Actuarial Prediction," 48–49

Status-degradation, in the courts, 122

Stereotyping, 120–21

Stigmatizing, use of, 31–32, 56, 118–26

Street, D., et al.: *Organization for Treatment,* 69

Subcommittee on Invasion of Privacy, 51–52

Subculture, delinquents as a, 89–90

Sutherland, Edwin H.:
Criminology, 87–88, 109
Professional Thief, 91

Szasz, Thomas S.: *Ideology and Insanity,* 41, 56

Tannenbaum, Frank: *Crime and the Community,* 119–20, 124

Theft, acts of, 13

Thrasher, Frederic M.: *The Gang,* 87

Toby, Jackson:
"Early Identification and Intensive Treatment Programs," 46, 47, 49, 50
"Social Disorganization," 160

Traditions, of delinquency, 87–88

Training schools (*see* Institutions)

Transition zones, in cities, 84, 86

Typologies, of delinquency, 13–17

Vested interests, of institutions, 134–35

Victim-blaming, 107

Victimless crimes, 144–45

Violence, on television, 109–10

Werthman, Carl: "Function of Social Definitions," 163

Will, role of, 138–39

Witter, Charles, 51–52

Wolfenden Report, 143–44

Working classes, and delinquency, 90, 92

Youth culture, and delinquency, 140–43

Youth Services Bureau, 63

Zald, Mayer: "Organizational 'Character,'" 65, 67